The Psychology of Your Stars

OrangeBooks Publication

Smriti Nagar, Bhilai, Chhattisgarh - 490020

Website: **www.orangebooks.in**

First Edition, 2021

ISBN: 978-93-90837-08-3

The opinions/ contents expressed in this book are solely of the author and do not represent the opinions/ standings/ thoughts of OrangeBooks.

Printed in India

THE PSYCHOLOGY OF YOUR STARS

NOT YOUR REGULAR
HANDBOOK OF ASTROLOGY

ARUN BABBER
MARINA KAMAL

OrangeBooks Publication
www.orangebooks.in

Contents

"Anyone can be a millionaire, but to become a billionaire you need an astrologer."

—J. P. Morgan

Warning

Starting out this book with a warning is not a war cry to scare you off. It is in fact a very closely thought out process to make one realise, that this book holds the power to transform one out of his/her lazy rug and pump up the dormant energies hidden inside. Once man is unleashed in his freedom, he is difficult to control, he becomes dangerous. And this danger is being shared here.

The book is not a work of fiction, so to reap the maximum benefit of transformation one must come back to it again and again, and it remains my sincere promise, that with each time one comes back to it, one would find a deeper meaning and a newer sense of perspective.

The book is initially spread into a brief understanding of astrology and the relation of the stars with our personal psyche. This relation is not a limiting belief to get one into believing astrology, but rather an outward call to become totally sceptic of what exactly one thought they knew about themselves. To question everything about what one thinks about themselves, to question ones talents, achievements, one successes and equally ones failures. And soon enough one would find the limiting perspectives one held in knowing their true self.

The book also unravels one of the rarest mythologies, which have been carefully selected to blow one's mind out of proportions and to hit the exact nerves which are required to be hit at the essential moments of life. The sequence of these short myths are hence very carefully put up to create havoc in one's mind in a sequential yet progressive manner.

So once again, I would re-iterate, one must take the steps ahead in his monkey mind with utmost caution, and the following chapters might as well break down what one once thought about themselves. For direct understanding of one's true self, the book in its final few chapters also reveals few generalized examples of nodular combinations.

If one really follows and experiences this book in their life, the virtual simulation that had been playing along for so many years might just drop some fortunate moment.

Good luck!

Karmic Astrology

One of the great psychologists of our time revealed in one of his discourses that the term personality is inadvertently misunderstood. The general and clichéd understanding of personality breaks it down to its etymology saying that personality is derived from the word 'persona' meaning a mask. And that's what the actors wear on the stage. So a person with a personality is just acting out his role which suits his unconscious or survival pursuits. This is very likely the reason that the self is not related to the personality, because the general perception of personality is very negative in the philosophical or humanitarian aspect. All the great spiritual leaders and thinkers talk against personality as something we should remove over ourselves as a mask is removed to bring out the real face behind the person.

The question that remains here is that why am I talking about the term personality while starting to make sense out of karmic astrology.

There is a source of deep secret in how the karmic debts of the past have a relation to the present life form by understanding the real meaning of the term personality.

Personality is at a crude level a basic formation of two major aspects of life, one aspect which remains to an extent unchangeable and the other which becomes always changing and impermanent. These two can be coined as attitudes and aptitudes respectively.

Attitudes are simply traits of the self that we are born with, the very genetic formation of our inner structure, which includes our physical mechanism and in turn governs our mental faculties.

Aptitudes are traits that are formed by the gradual changes of environment that happen upon us. This environment that a person is surrounded by is unique in its form, meaning no two people can ever have similar environments given to them, not even siblings, not even twins to say. The formations of the environment happens through the reception of the senses, and what we hear, see, touch, and smell can never be the same for two people.

These two aspects forever govern the way a man behaves in its unique way in this world.

Karmic astrology is a system of astrology that says we are born through a particular life form and we carry the learnings and mislearnings of the previous lifetime into this life. And in this lifetime we have to learn and repay through this junk that we have got underhand. This if taken metaphorically simply relates to a particular set of genes that we are born with and play these genes in a biological way to an approximate duration of 5 years of our lives, till the forces of this life or the aptitudes of this life start to have an effect on the behaviours of ourselves. And then with time behaviours are formulated, the mind starts to develop till the age of puberty, when another explosion happens to us in the form of volcanic impulses that make us animalistic in a way trying to figure out what do we need to do to keep our hungers met.

Man or woman through puberty find out that they have desires, and these desires need to be met or they would just not let us become fully capable human beings.

Many cultures have given books and talks on wisdom, ways of disciplines, only and only in the fear of the animalistic nature of human puberty.

Man forgets his past and is driven by the future in such a phase of his life. He forgets what he was, he just wants what he wants, and he starts living through his unlimited desires and the infinite source of energy that he feels within himself. This is what Joseph Campbell says is the

CALL FOR ADVENTURE. The man goes out on a mission to build his leather jackets and his lavish empires. He finds rocks and pebbles, in the form of trials and tribulations on the way.

But wait, where had his karmic debt, his past learning vanished suddenly? These are buried deep now. To uncover the hidden potential he needs to break out of the vanity of the unconscious and give way to the growth of the self-lurking deep within him.

To understand the workings of such two contradictory and opposing powers of the unconscious impulse and the conscious self within becomes the great mystery of his lifetime. Everyone lives this mystery in one way or the other. Everyone is trying to find out what they are meant to do, how they are meant to do it. Also, we want to know what we are not meant to do, and how we are to avoid it.

This source of information is hidden in the astrological chart of ours, and can be tapped through the knowledge of the karmic system of astrology.

Here comes the mention of the lunar nodes in the consequent chapter of this book. **The potential sources of great energies that guide our lives. The North Node(Rahu) and the South Node(Ketu).**

In karmic astrology it is believed that the south node carries the learnings of the past and the north node carries the trials of the future. So in a way we can say that the south node tells us what we are already good at, and the north node tells us exactly what we are supposed to learn and master in this lifetime to feel fulfilled.

This in turn brings a two way energy battle, as the north node and the south node are diametrically opposite on the chart, 180 degrees apart from each other. And in the interpretation of the houses they belong to, it clearly shows that the experiences are contradictory in their nature too.

Example, if the north node is placed in the 5th house then the south node is placed in the 11th house, if NN is placed in the 6th house, the SN is placed in the 12th house and so on and on.

The 5th house is the house of personal pursuits and the 11th house is the house of community service. Both having great contradictions to each other. The 6th house is the experience of distributing knowledge, the 12th house is the experience of gaining knowledge.

So when a person has already learnt and lived a life of giving knowledge, it becomes a great struggle to be able to attain a perception of learning. He was sitting on the teachers chair and now he is brought into becoming a student. A great ego clash, a great struggle of energies. And that is precisely what life is, an endless journey of inner conflicts and contradictions. And if this contradiction is not understood it can host a life full of turmoil, if understood it can bring upon a life of deep acceptance and satisfaction.

In this journey through this book, we are trying to discover and bring out a certain acceptance of the contradictory forces in action inside us, followed by the ways of integrating the learnings of our past with the trials of the future to bring out the highest potential of manifestation of these energies that combine to form the self.

Astrology And The Self Experiences Of Modern Day Life

The integration of astrology and the propositions of the self, remains the core aspect of this book. This book is meant to serve as an expansive material to understand the workings of the unique and individual self that works independently in it's behaviour and co-dependently in its association with other individuals and groups. This understanding has been historically made through psychology and philosophy in a two faced process, both denying each other's presence and belongingness to each other. This material hence serves to bridge the gap between science and its humorously illogical brother called philosophy/art.

Astrology is invariably an art form which prescribes infinite possibilities with each passing second of the energy cycle of the earth and its neighbouring forces. These forces linked to the movement of the planetary bodies around it and energy centres form the basis of understanding how the self is moving through a constant and dynamic flow of an immensely complicated process generally termed as life. So let's understand what these forces and the planetary bodies really are and how they correspond to ultimately understanding the self.

Lunar Nodes In Astrology

And as I mentioned earlier, there are other points of energies that are not planetary in their forms but centres of great energies called the North Node(Rahu) and South Node(Ketu). These astronomically denote the points of intersection of the paths of the Sun and the Moon as they move on the celestial sphere. Therefore, Rahu and Ketu are respectively called the north and the south lunar nodes. This will be later discussed in the way Rahu and Ketu form the basis of karmic astrology and the core centre of this entire material and revelating the hidden secrets of one's travels through his lives. So now we have for the starters of the understanding 12 energy cores that produce a sense of disturbance by their motion in the orbital planes thereby manufacturing different behavioural and intuitional alignments inside us.

Houses Of Astrology

Now let us come to the next terms called the houses. Precisely the western chart is a 360 degree circle divided into 12 equal parts. These 12 parts of 30 degrees are coined into what we call houses and give different set of experiences to the individual as per the planets that reside in them. So the combination of a planet inside a particular house defines a particular set of behaviour in the individual. These 12 houses can be taken as 12 ways in which life is experienced by the self. Starting from the first house these experiences are:

1 house (corresponding to Aries) - It starts from Ascendant. There is one's self, one's personal manifestations (mostly physical ones), 1st house often shows how one looks. Like Aries this house shows how exactly native is conquering the world, how native is establishing himself.

2 house (corresponding to Taurus) - Here we find one's talents, one's values (material and ethical). Native's money, properties (those that can be moved) his personal belongings, his income, his spending, his nutrition. Here we can see how energy comes to his body. Here will also be native's experience, his skills and talents in this or that. Crafting goes under 2 house too (not art though).

3 house (corresponds to Gemini) - Here we can see native's short trips and small travels, his communication, his brothers and sisters, his neighbors. This house is also responsible for speech, writing, small business and business qualities.

4 house (corresponds to Cancer) - one's tribe, environment, motherland, parent's house, parents, real estate. Here we find native's patriotic feelings, traditions of his land and his family, one's genetics.

5 house (corresponds to Leo) - here native is active and in the center of everyone's attention - acting, public speaking, sports. This house is also responsible for all that brings joy into ones life - hobbies, lovers, games and play, children.

6 house - (corresponds to Virgo) - service and work, not private business but working for someone. Here native often works for survival (not doing what he really likes).

This house is also responsible for one's health, it shows one's relationships with medicine, clinics, doctors etc. Here will also be small domestic animals, one' personal hygiene, household matters.

7 house (corresponds to Libra) - here will be natives one to one relationships - both: partners and enemies. Marriage, contracts, unions, collaborations and also one's ability to compromise.

8 house (corresponds to Scorpio) - house of transformation, death, sex, inherited money, credits, debts, large business projects, large sums of money. Here one finds dangers and his way to deal with them. Also this house is responsible for everything occult, magical. As well as for everything that is on the edge.

9 house (corresponds to Sagittarius) - travels, far away trips, higher education and scientific career, native's connections abroad. Here we find law. Here we also find our ideals, religions, gurus, our ways to understand world. Here we can see how God works in our lives.

10 House (corresponds to Capricorn) - Career, social calling, work that needs higher education, superior positions, politics, fame, respect, bosses. One's goals.

11 house (corresponds to Aquarius) - here one becomes humanitarian. Here he doesn't want anything for himself. Here he is selfless. Here we can see ones friend circle or social circle, his relationship with large groups. Often here we see astrologers. Here one is thinking of a perfect world, of future.

12 house (corresponds to Pisces) - house of God and everything that is hidden. Hidden services, activities. Secrets. Solitude. Sometimes forced (jail, mental institution, monastery).

The Yin And Yang of Our Personal Self

By the end of this chapter, we get a brief understanding of the various experiences one gathers or moves through in his lifetime. These all experiences must be related to the different houses that the planetary energies move through to better understand what is going to be revealed in later chapters. To understand the reality of one's self and how one precisely behaves in life is easier to grasp when one understands the energies or powers he is born with. What are his strengths and his weaknesses, what comes easy to oneself and what takes struggle, what brings unsolicited joy and what brings misery. This yin and yang provides the very firm grounding of one's contradicting nature and the struggles between ones comforts and ones goals. The struggle between being at home or travelling to far off places, the struggles of being selfish or being too nice to everyone. These contradictions are the core essence of the self and if realised as two sides of the same coin through direct experience of one's true self creates what Lao Tsu calls the automatic life. The life that flows like a river through the valleys and consorts various weathers and rocks and stones, it passes through various terrains unhindered and finally meets and melts in the high seas.

As a bee gathering nectar does not harm or disturb the color and fragrance of the flower; so do the wise move through the world.

– Gautam The Buddha

The Rahu-Ketu Story
Symbolism of The Nodes

The Puranas symbolise the story of the lunar nodes as the head and the body of a Asura(devil) cut into halves by the female form of the Lord Vishnu. The female form called Mohini, was sent upon the clash of the devils and gods in the samudra manthan, the churning of the milk ocean to bring out the nectar of immortality called Amrit.

Mohini is distributing the Amrit to all the gods (sitting in a queue). The Devil Swarbhanu is sitting in disguise with the gods so that he can drink a part of the Amrit, and before Mohini could sense the disguise, Swarbhanu already drank the Amrit. To Mohini's anguish, and to save the world from an immortal devil, Mohini cuts the head of Swarbhanu. The head and the body quickly start moving apart at a 180 degree separation from each other, with a curse from Mohini that they will never reform together. So, now one devil turns into two. They are Named Rahu(North Node) and Ketu(South Node). They both are on opposite ends, immortal yet ever separated. To understand this contradiction, vedic astrology says that Rahu and Ketu since then are held responsible for mans dual nature and the spiritual drama that ensues inside mans mind being nothing but this separated yet immortal aspect of the rahu-ketu story.

We also see in certain myths representing Rahu with the material and ketu with the spiritual. Hence, many of the modern day spiritual traditions are seen to be trying to formulate a way of life where the spiritual and the material meet in harmony. A certain truth of existense has been understood by such foundations and traditions, but out of their incomplete knowledge they are not able to understand the unique and special circumstances in which this duality exists inside the human mind.

The study of Astrology has been done in various traditions, the Buddhist traditions have researched this secret knowledge calling it the Kala-Chakra Tantra meaning the code behind the Wheel of time. Gautam Buddha after his detailed study into human psychology did understand the neuro-scientific behavior of man and his emotions by creating the meditative technique today known as Vipassana or in the west as Mindfulness, but also came to this conclusion, that the neuroscientific behavior is unique for all individuals, every man is entitled or accustomed to different emotions, some are by birth more aggressive, some by birth more peaceful, some are by birth more organized, some reckless. This sort of behavioral study needed more research to understand as to how and under what situation is a man born in, and why such differences are present inside humans and no other species. To this Budhha turned to more esoteric sciences of the Hindu cults and researched to form what he then called the Kala-Chakra, where he discusses the importance of the nodes by calling them the dragons head(North Node) and the dragons tail(South Node).

Gautam Buddha called this duality two parts of the same dragon, the same dragon Joseph Campbell frames as the one that one finds on the way to his adventure. The dragon finds man once he jumps out of his home, which astrologically happens at about 19 years of age, this is almost the time one faces his first dragons. The Later dragons will be discussed in detail in the subsequent chapters, the dragon of the middle age and the dragon of the age of wisdom.

Through this book and the lineage of karmic astrology this myth is being uncovered in a way that becomes more suitable to each individual life form. The ever haunting question of man to his craving passions and the societal pull that keeps him away from pursuing his dreams, his passions, his inner feelings can be seen and understood very clearly by understanding the position of ones nodes on the astrological chart.

The question comes now, we all know our zodiac as it has been inculcated in our primary educational entertainment through magazines and daily newpapers. But how do we know what our nodes are. We know ourselves as aquarius, cancerians, leos, scorpios etc but we do not know ourselves in terms of our nodes. This is not so very difficult to know, but a little homework has to be done to create our own personal birth charts on the western/vedic astrological map.

Keeping our date of birth, time of birth, and location of birth, we can easily create our western/vedic chart by any online means. Once the chart is prepared. It would look something like this.

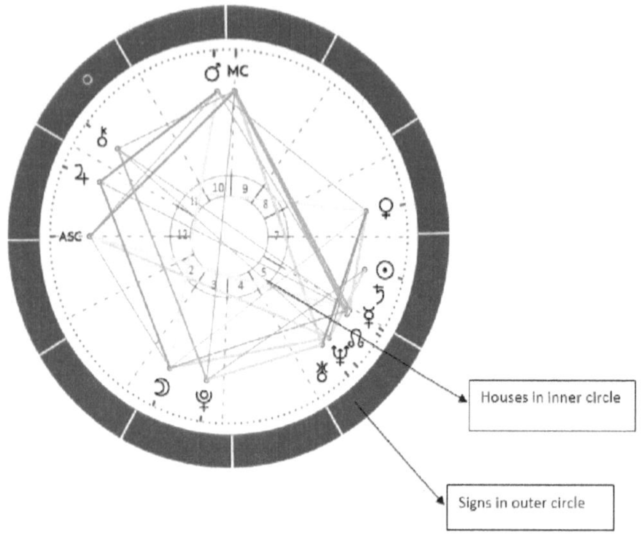

The position of planets in the chart shown above:

⊙ Sun in *16° 14' Aquarius*

☽ Moonin *4° 52' Scorpio*

☿ Mercury in *29° 26' Capricorn*

♀ Venus in *9° 10' Pisces*

♂ Marsin *4°21'Gemini*

♃ Jupiterin *7°35'Leo(r)*

♄ Saturnin *29° 51' Capricorn*

♅ Uranusin *11°45'Capricorn*

♆ Neptune in *15° 25' Capricorn*

 **Plutoin** *20° 17' Scorpio*

North Node in *27° 15' Capricorn* *(r)*

Chiron in *22° 48' Cancer* *(r)*

ASC **Ascendant in** *29° 18' Leo*

MC   **MC in** *27° 12' Taurus*

Lets not make you an academic astrologer here, but make it simple for the most layman reader, who may not be interested in astrology but is surely interested in the pursuit of his own life.

We are only interested here as of now in what we call the North Node or the Rahu, symbolized above in the chart by ☊. So how do we call ourselves through the Nodes? We simply are interested here as to which house the north node is situated and which sign it is holding.

The houses in the chart are written in numbers in the inner circle and the signs are written in the outer circle as shown in the figure above.

The above chart shows that the North Node is in the 5th House in Capricorn. We only now need to understand for this individual the characteristics of the 5th house and the behaviours of the Capricorn sign. This would entitle us to give this individual his social responsibility, broadly speaking the purpose or better said the flow of his life. Another thing imperative here is that the south node need not be seen in the chart. We know by now that the south node is always diametrically opposite to the north node, so the south node for this chart lies in the 11th house which is diametrically opposite to the 5th house and the sign with the 11th house here is the cancer.

So we have here now the duality of this individual, the 5th house with its Capricious nature is the direction of his social growth and his 11th house with its Cancerian nature is the direction which keeps him away from living the flow of his life.

The Spiritual drama entails now, the 11th house of the individual representing the loss of ego and service to the community is what the individual is born capable of and will again and again slip into such behavior, whereas his 5th house will want him to flourish his personal self, to create a beautiful attractive self, to be concerned with his image, his personal pleasures and his growth, to work on himself, but his mind will keep telling him to drop this foolish behavior and work for others. This conventional see-saw will keep this man engaged into a constant hustle in his mind. His capricious nature with his north node wants him to grow and establish himself, but his Cancerian nature in his south node will want him to serve the needy forgetting about his personal goals. This is a short and very brief example of one of the many dualities that exist in different charts and in reality in the minds of different individuals. Later in this book we will discuss and reform more articulately the different combinations of such node combinations both in houses and signs, to make a detailed investigation into all the possible permutations that will fit into one of your own personal charts.

To accept some idea of truth without experiencing it, is like a painting of a cake on paper which you cannot eat.

– Suzuki Roshi

Rahu And Ketu The Principle Of The Nodes.

The way we have already understood that nodes are represented in Indian mythology and astrology as Rahu and Ketu, two parts of the same body, eternally separate but always wanting to come together to become immortal once again. This same way we will take upon here the behaviours and attributes of these two nodes, namely the north node also represented by Rahu – the head and South node represented by Ketu - the body.

What has to be understood here that when we take upon an astrological chart through the study of nodes, then it is far more subtle and intricate than studying the sun sign of an individual. When we study the sun sign of an individual, we study the personality of a particlar sign that belongs to the sun of that persons chart. So we compare now the personality of that sign with that of the native. Let's say for example when we say that the native is a sun sign Leo, then we are typically thinking of the lion, we symbolize this person with an affinity towards pride, towards costly cars and shiny watches, superior sense of clothing and an authoritative stance in social environments. He will be the centre of the room with his stories of overwhelming wealth and class. That is typically how we describe the native through his sun sign.

But this is typically not how we understand the purpose of our individual lives and the conflicts arising in trying to fulfill it. This is studied through the action and the position of the nodes in the persons chart. Hence to understand how to work with the nodes, we have to first understand the principle on which the nodes function and then apply it to our personal charts, through the ways described in earlier chapters through which we recognise our nodes.

Rahu – Principle of the North Node.

The head representing the north direction, the way of moving up, but something which is beyond reach at the moment. Rahu is something far away at the moment but something we have our hands towards, something so close yet so far. Rahu is an earthly desire to fulfill, to be what we are not yet but what we see around and feel most inspired by. This is not something that our televisions or our instagrams tell us, but a very true desire to be what we feel is around us. The child looks at his father and gets inspired by not what his father is, but by what his inner feeling wants him to desire, he only sees that. A north node in Aries will only see how his father fights against the odds to bring up his family with great comfort. A north node in Leo will only see his father telling stories in the middle of the congregation of friends, he will see him laugh, play dance and sing in parties. A north node in capricorn will see his father working hard to build his career, his professional goals, burning midnight oil to be the best he can be.

The child looks around in the world and mirrors the desires of his inner calling, ie to say his North node. He keeps working towards this, the nerdy one studies, he doesn't know why, the flirty one hangs around the opposite sex, he doesn't know why too. As kids we often live through our desires without prejudice but as we grow up our personal desires are lost in the collective desires of the society and we get confused as to who is really living on the right pattern, then we try to imitate them. We look for answers within our parents, our teachers, our friends, our colleagues, our moviestars and our political heroes, and we try to find out where the right way of life resides, failing to realise that the right way is right within. Through the study of the nodes, we can definitely come back to realising our true nature, our true desires, and our true potential.

The north node out of all this can simply be understood of being the domain of our true desires, through which we fulfill our lives with contentment and satisfaction.

Ketu – Principle of the South Node.

The body away from the head, the big heap of mass, the weight on our legs and the heaviness of our hearts. In the south node lies eveyrthing that we carry, it is the burden of our soul that we carry from all our previous experiences that we bring upon here as our primary material to work with this life.

The south node brings to us our personal character, the way we behave and climb the mountain of our childhood and transit into our youth is through the powers of our south node. We live with humour, or with intelligence or with courage in our school days is only an accumulation or the wired genetic pattern that we symbolically here call the south node.

Here is the trick of the nodes, just as we transit through our chilhood to our youth is the time when the desires of our life burgeon and are seen to be very separate from what we already are. It is foolish and illogical to desire something we have in our hands, and it is absolutely true to desire something we do not have yet in our hands. So what we have here in our hands is our south node and what we want is our north node. This is the great dilemma of the impulsive youth and its heroics. We stumble, fall and rise because we want something that we don't have yet, although having our hands already full with a burden as large as the symbolism of our south node. The south node is heavy, it's a burden of a whole body, the north node is a small fruit the size of a melon in the form of the head. But this very melon keeps us wanting for more and more till we quench our thirsts.

To understand and accept this conflict is the primary way of finding clairvoyance inside our very being, through the study of these opposites we find within ourselves a great battle. A battle of opposing energies symbolised in different cultures by different images and philosophies. But the core conflict inside our beings remains this, and till it doesn't get sorted and accepted it keeps lurking around and manifesting itself in the form of anxieties and frustrations, in fears and guilts. To break through the barriers of this duality, the acceptance of our true powers (Ketu) and our true desires (Rahu) is a monumental step in the complete fulfillment of the natives life.

For things to reveal themselves to us, we need to be ready to abandon our views about them.

– Thích Nhat Hanh

Indras Palace
The Brahmavar Upanishad

The patron of the gods, born as the mighty king of thunder, Indra has grown up to be a great leader of sorts. With time watching over him, a great devil named rudra falls upon the earth creating havoc all around the place. He stops the rivers from flowing and suddenly, the entire earth is draught struck. Indra is called upon to take matters in his hand, after bewildering for a while, he finds a box of thunder bolts in his pocket, throws one at rudra turning him into ashes. The whole world blooms again, flowers raining on the marvelous victory of Indra. Indra is on cloud nine with an overwhleming sense of achievement. Victory fills him with such pride, he wants to feel the very essence and the profoundness of his great powers. And like any middle aged man, who has climbed the ladders of success in the workplace battling his own rudras, Indra now feels showing it off in terms of his lavish rides, to which the corporate leader would buy a big SUV or a shining sedan. If that was not much, they want a lavish house, beautiful interiors, leather sofas, extravagant chandeliers, modular kitchens, so does Indra wants a palace of his own. The greatest palace that has ever been.

Indra calls upon the architect of the gods, Vishwakarma. He asks Vishwakarma to build the most beautiful and grand palace that has ever been built on the top of the cosmic mountain. Vishwarama turns into action soon, and within no time the palace comes into being. Indra is called upon for the inspection of the palace. Although the palace being like no other, but that doesn't sort out the overwhelming desires of indra, he wants more. He gives his list of further augmentations to the palace, making it even more grandiose. Vishwakarma starts over on his work again, and again in no time, he fulfills all the wishes of Indra and even more. Indra comes again for the inspection, and gives even more points to add on. Vishwakarma is irritated now, he feels he is stuck for life, while he feels in his head that there is no end to the desires of this Indra. He feels this is a never ending loop. What do I do now Vishwakarma shouts out in pain. Lord Brahma, the manifestor of the cosmos appears in front of him and asks him, Son what makes you weep?

Vishwakarma says, I am stuck for life, I have build the most beautiful palace ever built in history but the desies of Indra are never ending. The white collar man bought a beautiful mercedes, but in a week he wants an upgrade, he changes the interiors, he finds decals for the doors, then a better stereo, then a bass amplifier and what not, the cravings are never ending.

Brahma assures vishwakarma that he will sort Indra out by showing him the reality of his illusory pride, and asks him to go back home and sleep peacefully.

Next morning, outside the palace of Indra visits a beautiful blue eyed boy, filled with glare on his cheeks and a smile on his face. He is dancing and singing as the villagers look at him in absolute awe and admiration. Never before has been seen a boy as beautiful as him. Indra hears of the boy and calls him to his court. Indra asks the blue eyed boy, what brings you here pretty boy?

The boy with his cheeky smirk says that, I have been roaming this cosmic mountain for milleniums but never have I ever seen any Indra before you, build a palace as beautiful as this one.

Indra is mouth open, he says, what do you mean by **Indras Before?** The boy says yes, I have never seen any indra before you build such a beautiful palace before. I have seen hundreds of indras come and go but you are the the fiercest. And I foresee that the higher the rise, the greater will be the fall.

He takes indra for a walk, and on the way they see an army of ants and the boy smiles again. Indra has his toes on his heads, and ask why do u smile little boy looking at these ants. The boy says, only ask if you are prepared to be hurt. Indra says go on, I want you to teach me.

The boy says, **they are all previous Indras**. Every time an Indra comes and the world is in shivers and he kills a rudra, the Indra says oh what a great king am I and boom he falls into the grounds of the lowest manifestations of the cosmos(ants) and then lifetimes before he again becomes priviledged to be an Indra, and then again a rudra is killed and then again he says, oh what a great king am I, and boom again he falls.

Indra falls on his knees, he calls vishwakarma and asks him to stop the work on the palace and frees him of his duties.

The white collar man rises to the heights of his pride without understanding that this too is another manifestation of the principles of the cosmic energies. He is not playing the game, the game is being played upon him. He is not the director of the show, he is merely an actor of this great cosmic play called the Leela.

The north node calls upon few men to be leaders (10th house), to become great entertainers, to   shine in life (5th house), to build great wealth (2nd house), to become great reformers/teachers   (8th house), to find the knowledge of the gods (12th house) but all of this is simply but the manifestations of the ultimate in different forms. There is nothing really to feel proud about but to realise what we are meant to be and just simply be that. To realise ones true potential is not a matter of achievement but a matter of great inner fulfillment, which leaves mans with no outer desire due to the complete inner contentment of finding his true purpose and living by it. This is where the society fails today in not providing the relevant myths to man to find his centre and rest in it.

Indra rests in his peace of being a true patron of the gods, and fulfills each of his duties henceforth with sobriety and pure dedication.

Silence is the respite of the confident and strong.

-Ryan Holiday

The Story Of Hanuman
The Dragon Of Youth

There exists one of the most interesting myths in Indian history that represents the exact knowledge of the unconscious through the story of the immortal and celibate God Hanuman. Before we get down to the actual myth we must understand the personality of this God that will form the essence of this relevant myth here.

Hanuman was born with an extremely powerful personality, could might have well be confirmed with his birth chart, but no such detail exists in the story. To this bright and charismatic boy, troubles were sure to ensue. This was well understood by Hanuman's parents as well as by the gods looking upon him from the open skies. With each passing year hanuman was growing more and more powerful, and his childfull curiosities were making him check his powers in all ways that he could possibly avail.

This is exactly how our pubic ages make us participate in life, the masculine hits hard and we want to prove our mettle, we arm wrestle with our friends, we want to take upon physical fights, we want to ride bikes and drink bottles of beer, the feminine too is not free of this enormous energy, it wants to go out on the most adventurous romances, make out in extremely inappropriate places, want to make lovers who are genuine assholes. This sort of impulsive rage takes over both the feminine and the male energies in their life form regardless of the gender that they are working upon.

Coming back to hanuman, he went out in his naughty adventurous, so much so as to look upon the sun and have a desire to eat it like a candy. He flies towards the sun and approaches it in supersonic speeds to see that it kept on increasing in its size the closer he got to it, but Hanuman's will and his understanding of his power doesn't make him take a step back, he keeps approaching the sun with his full might. Looking at Hanuman's determination, the gods are worried, and the most worried is the sun god, who thinks this is the end of his existence. The gods call upon the help of the King of god's, the Great Indra, residing over his crown on his magnificient elephant Airavat, the elephant with seven trunks. Indra throws his mightiest weapon on hanuman and it hits hanuman on his chin, making him fall flat unconscious. As he falls down on earth, a Great crater is formed with the weight of Hanuman's might. The gods worried as to the prophecies that hanuman was meant to fulfill and come together to grant him another life with even greater powers, the boon of immortality henceforth and an exceptional power to disguise and change forms on will.

Although defeated in his task to eat up the sun, Hanuman is enthralled with his new powers and takes upon another adventure in his intellectual prowess now. He goes on to ask questions to the intellectual Brahmins and yogis of the land and disturbs them to their might. Hanuman's intelligence far beyond the grasp of the mortal yogis and their failure in answering him irritates their deepest cores. They all come together and curse him to forget all his powers and boons that he had been blessed with. The amazing thing to note here is that the curse mentions **forgetting the powers** and not losing them. The curse also follows that hanuman will only remember these powers when a man capable enough would come along in his life to remind him of what he really is. Hanuman strives to live henceforth as a normal mortal and struggles in his basic chores of life. He had forgotten everything and is working upon life step by step, moment by moment now.

This is the story of the human problem at the end of pubic youth, the end of adolescence can make even the brightest, sharpest and most intelligent men/women go astray. And when life hits them with its basic chores, they are left with nothing but empty souls and anxious heads. The pursuit of money, jobs, marriage and family can eat even the most valiant men raw and alive. That is exactly what happened with hanuman. But the real nature of a man does not die, it just lurks beneath the whole circle of life waiting for a small revelation which is given to him by someone in the role of a master, a teacher or a guru.

The north node with its enormous powers is forgotten in the middle of innocence and vanity, with great perseverance it is enriched again by someone who comes along during the phase of life when one is fighting his trials and working upon his struggles. The north node has to be understood here of having a complete cycle of 19 years. Funny, it is exactly the last age of the teens, of the age of adolescence. Now the second cycle ensues man with another 19 years, this is the period when one needs the highest perseverance and patience. These nineteen years define if man is going to find out his true nature, if he is going to find out what the north node demands of him or not, and the most successful men are those who break out of the chains of the unconscious in the second cycle of the north node. And this is exactly the reason that most successful men come out in public in their forties, coz they have now become fully capable and in tune with their north node. Their sense of clarity and direction in life is unshaken now and their will to live upon exactly as the demands of their true nature is strong as an axe.

Nothing new happens to hanuman too, in the midst of his great meditation practice that he has taken upon to still his mind, he one fine day meets the mortal God Ram, who is in search of his lost wife in the woods. On looking at Hanuman, Ram is certain that this is no ordinary man and asks upon his help. Hanuman oblivious of his powers, still binds his promise to help Ram in whatsoever way he can. What hanuman was unaware of at this moment, was that his help was going to turn out into the road towards his ultimate freedom into his true nature. Ram in the journeys ensuing this event, gradually reminds hanuman of each of his powers to the point that Hanuman becomes his greatest soldier in the army that would lead to the resurrection of the lost humanity in the land of India. Hanuman becomes the decisive power that leads Ram to victory over the Devil King Raavan who is found out to have kidnapped Ram's wife.

This sort of the return of man back to his true nature is common point in all myths and ultimately in all lives. One has to move through the years of his unconscious development and its connected vanity. One has to then face the odds of conscious living when the hangover of the poison of his unconscious hits him hard on his face. The return does not happen with suppressing ones unconscious but to wait and be aware of the inner energies that are binding one to refrain from entering into his real direction. One waits and waits till he finds someone who reminds him again of what his capabilities are, and in the following years one also becomes the same reminder in someone else's life. This automated software keeps the science of evolution in place and consciousness keeps evolving at its intended pace through this cosmic game.

The question of whether or not there is a God or truth or reality or whatever you like to call it, can never be answered by books, by priests, philosophers or saviours. Nobody and nothing can answer the question but you yourself, and that is why you must know yourself - Immaturity lies only in total ignorance of self.

- *Jiddu Krishnamurti*

Manifestations Of The North Node
Budhhas Astrological Chart

The north node in its very core poses a serious problem, of not letting us know the quality of our direction, it does not really give us the right answer to exactly what are we really meant to do with this quality.

The answer to this is fairly hidden and only few individuals with excessively refined minds can see this in their lives.

The story of Gautam the Buddha is a brilliant example of this loss of clarity on the birth chart of an individual.

It is said that when Gautam the Buddha was born, him being a royal prince, it was indeed a great event in the erstwhile kingdom. His father brought upon the greatest astrologers to make his birth chart as precise as possible. His birth chart was made, and it was clear that he was no ordinary man. His north node was conjunct with large energies in the 10th house - the house of career. 10th house is also the house of leadership qualities. So it was very clear that the prince was on his way of becoming a great and profound king who will remembered for generations to come. But what does history tell us? This did not manifest.

Some rare astrologers also predicted that the Buddha who was named Siddharth then, would dwell into the depths of the human mind and formulate the very core principles of the functions and actions of the mind. But what did this mean in having a strong 10th house.

This mistake of treating the qualities of leadership only in one conventional perspective was how the greatest of the great astrologers faulted at. Buddha did ultimately lead, but what did he really lead?

That would remain unknown for so many years. When the Buddha renounced his princely affairs and left for the jungles, his birth chart seemed to fail. Astrology seemed to fail. But astrology never fails, make this very certain an understanding. Astrology is the code of God, it is the very basic software on which the cosmos functions. If this kind of faith is not appreciated in astrology, then it only remains a game to play and not the essence of directing the course of life as per the very laws of nature.

So eventually Astrology did not fail with Buddha either, he dwelled upon the deepest cores of the human mind, and found out the very truths about human existence, ultimately becoming the leader of not just a small kingdom but of the entire spiritual thirst of generations to come. So what manifested in his chart was even bigger than being a great king remembered for a few generations in a particular topography, instead he really became the worlds greatest spritual leader of his times and is still today. It was not then that the Hindus considered him the 9th avatar of Vishnu, but centuries later they had to give this prophecy to him.

Similarly, the north node can be similar for millions of people, but the manifestations can be absolutely unique. To understand one's own manifestations, one has to look 180 degree opposite to the south node and find out his powers that he already has access to. The south node will now help the north node to manifest. This is a very important statement to realise.

The south node helps the north node but keeps the mind coming back to the pleasures of the south node. The south node will keep pulling one back to enjoy its rewards but the real reward lies in the manifestation of the north node.

The south node is comfort, the north node is struggle. And man always keeps lurking around comfort, almost always trying to sleep over his issues. Almost always trying to avoid his struggles and find a loophole. South node is the loophole.

The south node will now help the north node to manifest. This is a very important statement to realise.

"This whole existence is a meeting of many dimensions. That is its beauty, its variety, and its unending process of celebration"

-OSHO Rajneesh

Samudra Manthan The Churning Of The Ocean

To figure out the two way energy battle that occurs inside the human head, a beautiful myth has been in place in ancient Indian literature. It sprouts up from the Vishnu Purana, but has rarely been understood out of its literal context. The metaphorical context of this deep mythology has been rendered useless by the degradation of the intellect in the Indian society with centuries of slavery through the hands of the foreign invaders.

So what do we have here, a great event between the Devas(the godly people) and Asuras(the evil people). This is not a battle between the two, let this be the first understanding. This is an event where the Devas and the Asuras come together to churn the ocean with Mount Mandara as the churning pillar and Vasuki(the king of serpeants) as the churning rope to find the immortality nectar called the Amrit.

But amrit is the deepest hidden treasure in the ocean and before it can be released, there come forth many other rewards/dangers including a poison named hala hala. If and only if the people involved in the churning are not seduced by the rewards and not shaken by the dangers, only then can they continue churning to reach the final stage where the amrit comes out of the Ocean.

This is essentially a mental struggle that we all posses, the pillar of morality is churning by the rights and wrongs on both sides in an attempt to find the rewards of life. We continuously struggle in our heads in this fashion, sometimes the white is winning and sometimes the black, but only if both come together and churn in harmony is when life grows with its rewards.

To find rewards in the form of desire fulfillment the churning has to keep going. And to find the ultimate reward of life one has to be what the ancient Greeks called the stoic. The stoic is unmoved by joy and sorrow and submits without complaint. Then what is the stoic doing here, he is simply experiencing both the joys and the sorrows with equal understanding. He is neither overwhelmed by the experience of joy nor is he in resentment with the experience of sorrow. He simply lives through it in perfect harmony of the conflicting energies that forever churn his mental and emotional processes.

The north node and the south node are something like the Devas and the Asuras here. They demand not a battle but a harmonious teamwork to keep alive the churning of life. But the criticality of this kind of a harmonious commitment is to understand that the south node is already fully developed, it is the power that we already posses and the north node is something that we need to conquer, that we need to formulate inside us. So the battle will always start with the Asuras with higher power, like mentioned in the story.

The story starts with the Asuras completely destroying the Devas with the leadership of their devil god Bali, taking over the reins of the universe. The Devas now approached Vishnu(the creator of the universe) in an attempt to regain their lost kingdom. But vishnu tells that a straight face to face battle will only lead them more destroyed and hence the Asuras are to be dealt with in a diplomatic way, by using their impulsive nature always in want of more. The Devas propose the churning of the Ocean to them and the possibility of amrit at the end of it. They discussed that the rewards will be divided equally and the amrit at the end is left for battle. Similarly in life, the Devas will be the underdogs when the fight initiates. But slowly they will graduate, they will work upon their strengths and build themselves one point at a time. This happens by careful precision in handling our impulses and being even friends with our enemies till when the time asks for.

The north node is hence our direction of work, the south node is the direction of how we keep our impulses intact with our already mastered qualities.

To keep our pride pressed through what we already are good at, and to focus our energies in what more we need to learn in life is the way to bring forth the amrit in our lives.

The South node brings forth the challenges of the ego, the north node brings forth the challenges of hard work. With the south node and its existing qualities we may go astray by just being ballooned in its pride, and let comfort seep in and say, what more do I need to learn, I am already great.

With the north node comes struggle, comes a demand for perseverance and day to day hustle. There comes a demand for rigorous self discipline in learning what we don't know yet, and for this we have to scratch underneath our very core, we need to remove the eyeliners to see clearly.

Are we willing to go till the end to find amrit or will we be left astray by the smaller rewards in the journey. This is the question that many avoid.

"We seldom realize, for example that our most private thoughts and emotions are not actually our own. For we think in terms of languages and images which we did not invent, but which were given to us by our society."

— Alan Watts

The Misery Of Society Man As The Omnivorous Animal

There needs to be a very fine understanding of the misery that societal expectations puts one into by realising that certain experiences are more favoured by the society such as the possession of wealth, higher education, great careers and higher positions, although it is not always true that these experiences might be the right ones for us. What is very clear here is that society has a narrow channel through which it sees what it takes to be successful and what it takes to be a failure in life, although reality says something else.

What reality is trying to tell us through the study of astrology is to understand the right ways in which one is supposed to lead his life and to understand the inner feelings of the self through careful examination of our masteries and our weaknesses. This would form the basis of understanding the self through astrology and remain the prime foundation of the entire material of this book. Astrology as a form of fortune telling and future predictions as a general conception about this intricate artform is not really the goal of us here. The goal is to get into the depths of oneself and to bring out a clear picture of what is right and what is wrong for us. This understanding will remain unique for each individual and will serve not as a theoretical representation into some tabular form but an acute understanding of the individual self which is both unique in its core and intersecting with various other individuals at the same time.

And to understand in its very depth the omnivorous nature of the man in such a chaos of societal life we must consider certain straight facts of life that bring us into eclectic wonder but soon wipe out from our minds.

We wonder sometimes how we really broke out of the food chain and got ourselves into the great chaos of civilization today. How is our survival different now, what makes us lesser animals, or what makes us more human than when we were in the jungle and its vast darkness.

In the jungle if seen closely, two types of major survival methods exist, at least at the macro level. The differentiation of these two types of methods is termed by biologists as herbivores and carnivores. This is what precisely shows us how certain species choose their eating habits or to say in turn their survival habits. On the surface it might seem that the herbivores have an easy life, they don't have to hunt for food, and their food is naturally docile and does not perform any repulsion in giving itself to the hungers of the moving animals. Whereas it looks on the surface that the great challenges are for the carnivores who have to constantly struggle and fight and kill for food.

The survival strategies for the herbivores include precise alertness through its senses and individual intelligence it has for its species. The monkey climbs the trees to save itself, the gazelle can run for miles without rest, and similarly all herbivores have their own set of skills to survive the attack. For the carnivores hence the food(herbivore) is not docile, it presents a challenge, it presents a particular intelligence and skill which they naturally cannot counter directly, so they need different skills like stealth, like finding weak spots in the herd, also night vision. They have evolved by developing these skills to counter the weaknesses of the herbivores: their moving- intelligent food.

The carnivore how much ever cruel it may seem on the wildlife documentary, it really is having a tough time, the lions have a hunt to kill ratio of 10:1, the polar bear has a 3:1, the leopard has a 4:1. Hence you cannot see a scene in which a lion is killing a small weak buffalo and decide on your personal humanistic moral grounds as to who is right and wrong here. You cannot call the predator cruel, when nature is itself cruel to him. You cannot call the herbivore weak when it is enjoying the luxuries of being weak. These are all personal apprehensions that have no concrete value in reality.

When we now come to the human survival problem, then one thing becomes very clear by looking at the history of all civilizations. Human civilization starts with the carnivorous instinct and as the civilizations develop it turns herbivores, not in its eating habits but in its lifestyles. Initially tribes runs over luxury seated cities, plunder it and out of it form their own cities, then slowly the cruelty comes down and they start organizing things, both man and material. It turns more and more herbivorous to the extent that another carnivorous tribe comes and plunders it all. This cycle goes on.

So the entire human problem lurks around the situation where man is unable to strike a combination of both skills at once, which is very hard to obtain. To be both carnivorous and herbivorous at the same time, hence to become omnivorous not by eating habits but by his very survivalist approach. To have the courage to fight adversity: to kill and find its own food and also to have sharp alertness to avoid anyone taking advantage of his luxurious state. This state of omnivorous skill is hard to obtain and hence civilizations rise and fall and the cycle goes on and on.

Man over the course of his life starts his independent life as a carnivore hence, finding a job, killing and stepping on people to reach where he expects a luxurious life, a life of no more killings and fighting. After his course of carnivorous encounters he finally settles to an individually decided level of comfort, every man has different ambitions, the more ambitious a man the higher level of comfort he wants to settle with. But the irony here is that the more ambitious one is, the lesser time in life he will find to live in comfort, for the reward of the quality of comfort he pays the price for the quantity(time) of his comforts. Some people retire early, more herbivorous. Some people work till their last breath, completely carnivorous. Only the few intelligent ones know when to switch their roles, from predator to cattle, and then in emergent situations from cattle to predator again and they choose this with their acute sense of self awareness. Some people become compulsive on their herbivorous instinct and choose to live like a monk, some become compulsive on being carnivorous and choose to play the game of power and money till their last breath. Both are compulsive, no one is better than the other. Only the one who first learns both the skills and then has the complete mental freedom to choose whatsoever fits in each situation of life lives fulfilled, lives moment to moment, lives in the here and now. This man with both the skills and the freedom to choose anyone of them is the awakened man.

So it is not difficult to understand here how symbolically it is being tried to re iterate the South Node and the North Node, through the story of the omnivorous animal. The South Node of comforts vs the North Node of challenges. The herbivore vs The Carnivore. Hence the realization that both exist together in harmony in bringing out the essential fulfillment of life.

"The purpose of life is finding the largest burden that you can bear and bearing it."

— Jordan B. Peterson

The Purpose Of Life
Burning Of The Soul

All your religious preachers, your spiritual masters, your psychotherapists, your teachers and parents and every wise man in the world from Lao Tzu to Socrates have forever denied answering this serious question. This kind of a mind wobbling denial about this question regarding the purpose of individual life has forever haunted even the greatest of intellectuals and the fiercest of warriors. Like Achilles says in the movie Troy, let me tell you something that they don't teach you in the temples.

So let me tell you something that your wise men are afraid of answering. Let me tell you the story of your life, the purpose, the mission, the goal, the aim of your very personal existence. I will not fray upon or be scared to use these very words that have been condemned by all the wise and holy masters all around the globe. I recently heard an Indian spiritual guru trying to evade this question by saying that, Life has no purpose. This acts as a kind of mental relaxment or a psychosomatic drug, by trying to release the burden of this great ever haunting question. But this is only an attempt of cowardice, not an attempt at living life in persistent clairvoyance and confidence. This answer can definitely make one enjoy their weekends but will definitely not let us live our weekdays. This is denial in its pure form.

The purpose of individual life is difficult to uncover, as it is not to be formulated by a set theory, it being wholistically unique for each and every individual. But what is unique for the psychologist, is also hideously similar in its patterns. The overall combination of a set pattern of drives can truly have infinite permutations, but if the individual patterns can be studied, then the unique resultant pattern can be uncovered quite possibly. This remains here the prime aim of this book.

To uncover the purpose of individual life forms by understanding certain set patterns and codes designed to work inside man for the gradual but constant evolution of consciousness in the cosmos is a very possible pursuit. What is needed here is a person who is ready, willing and courageous enough to discover his true self through constant enquiry and deep self observation in every pursuit of life that happens upon him. A person with a higher sense of self awareness and deep observation skills is required here, to have a grasp of this material and its slow but penetrating influence on self-understanding. The father of Indian astrology, has quoted in his astrological bible; 'Only the self-aware person can reap the fruits of astrology'. The self-loathing, impulsive and easily influenced person will only be interested in knowing when he will find a job and how hot his partner will be.

Predictive astrology is not the goal of this book, rather what is being developed here is a silent revolution against the predictive aspects of astrology which although maybe correct in their theory and application but have a direct and negative effect on the overall mental functioning of the native. Predictive astrology hits at the lowest forms of the mind, feeding on its trivial desires and fears. Predictive astrology how much ever a work of genius is really a waste of time and effort. This conviction will be found in each chapter in this book and will steadily kill the impulses that do not let man find out what will provide him true fulfillment. We all talk about what may give us true inspiration and fulfillment but when it comes out in finding our very personal core we try as much as possible in evading this discomfort. We watch a rockstar movie, and how the protagonist rebels against society to become what he truly was meant to be. We go home and we also want to play the guitar. Next weekend we see a movie of an artist, again being a failure at school and academics and rising against the odds to become what his true inner feeling wants it to be. So now we go home and order some paints, brushes, a canvas. And there it is, we fall again. We are overwhelmed by the feeling of fulfillment which we feel by looking at someone who has really found his purpose, but when it comes to finding our own, we are only limited to imitating these legends. We all hoot and shout at the best athletes, at the best comedians, and filmstars and politicians and entertainers, we admire great scientists that grew hair like a porcupine in trying to fulfill their inner most curiosities. But we only act like audiences when we are to look upon ourselves, we are afraid to get onto the stage.

That is the end of our wills and the genesis of our collective unconscious. With this book comes an opportunity to find out what we really are hidden inside this luring and self loathing layers of the collective and societal unconscious. This presents an opportunity as well as a possibility to believe in our inner feeling and to truly live through our hearts and souls.

"A system of morality which is based on relative emotional values is a mere illusion, a thoroughly vulgar conception which has nothing sound in it and nothing true"

— Socrates

The Question Of Morality One Pillar Of Righteousness

The question of having a single book or single pillar of righteousness remains a very common goal of most of the religious sects, especially the abrahamic ones. This seems to be right on the surface as to give humanity some sort of rules and guidance to live life through. So the question here is not about righteousness, the question here is about how to live a fulfilled life and such fulfillment is only brought out through living a life of balance, not very difficult to see how every small atom in the universe is trying to move towards a state of equilibrium, so is man trying to come into a state of equilibrium by balancing its conflicting energies.

This becomes now the very root of the understanding as to why the south node is being restricted in development in the study of karmic astrology, the south node is not immoral for a person to live by, it is simply a part of the personality which has been overly developed and the balancing side been neglected for a large period of time in the history of that soul or lets say the wave of energy. Hence a man who has constantly lived in the service of others has neglected his own personal happiness, his own personal pusuits in the long run of living for others, this man will need to live for himself, howsoever society calls him selfish. His morality will be turned upside down and he will have to face the odds of being treated as a selfish egoistic individual. But this is exactly not how it turns out to be with him, when he does start to live through his north node, to say for himself, it turns out that all this was in reality only a fear residing in his heart. When he does turn out to live for himself, he starts getting appreciation, he starts being applauded and appreciated for becoming the centre of the social circle on which people can rely upon. He starts to be looked upon by people for advice, for support for help and for dependance, he becomes the man whom people look upto during crisis.

The south node presents a definite fear in the individual for not being able to live thorugh the opposite end. He becomes reluctant, he starts fearing consequences of living on the other shore, the shore he has never seen, the unknown territory. This unknown territory is what joseph campbell very beautifully enumerates in one of his quotes, he says, **the cave you fear to enter holds the treasure you seek**. How much more beautifully can this truth of life be said, but the question comes to us as to which is the cave that holds our treasure. This direction that leads us to the cave is hidden in the sign and the house that our north node resides in. The palace of our comfort is directed by the sign and the house our south node resides in.

This sort of an understanding leads us to a self experiment, this experimentation has to start at some point of time, and by experience and through the study of human behaviour it can be said that such time in life generally happens during the mid of the second cycle of the nodes. One cycle of the node is of 19yrs approximately. Hence at the age of 19, our north node sprouts up and the inner conflict starts, and man sees that he is being pushed to unknown territories and unknown places and faces. He struggles to understand this phenomenon, and an average intellect takes about half of the next cycle, ie about 9-10 years to completely get on track with his north node, the more exceptionally intelligent the man is the sooner he will find out the balance and the more lethargic and cowardly a person is, he will keep delaying this balance.

We will in the consequent chapters see through the symbolism of few myths, the encounters and life sutuations that make us understand the quality and duration of such conflicts in our life. The way we react to such situations and the way to come out of them. Hence it is relevant here to mention that the myths must be taken not on a literal account but as a symbolism to uncover the feel of them. Myths need not be understood in a way we learn our academic subjects, but may be felt as a fictious story which creates a feel of the environment that the story takes us into. A myth must be read as if we watch a movie, just simply enjoying the characters and living thorugh their eyes for a brief moment in a theatre.

"There are two tragedies in life. One is to lose your heart's desire. The other is to gain it"

— George Bernard Shaw

Matsya Purana
The Never Ending Desires

The Matsya Purana like the Noahs Ark states a transition of one form of creation which is experiencing destruction to another which is experiencing creation. The journey happens in a boat when god tells his story to the deserving few, so when the new creation takes place, these few deserving individuals can set forth a new life form with the same laws of nature that he works with.

Manu starts his journey of being a well knowledgeable brahmin, brahmin meaning the one who has the knowledge of the brahma(the creator). Manu is not a particular man, there are manus in each Yuga of life. Each with the same purpose to set forth the new life that happens after the world closes its eyes.

So here in this story, Manu is taking his regular bath in the river nearby his small cottage, when he comes out with another dip, he notices in his hands a fish(**matsya**) who is crying for help. Manu asks matsya, what is that you want, what you are crying for. Matsya answers, it cannot stay in the river and requests to be taken out and brought to his home, Manu takes the fish in his earthen vessel and brings it home. When he wakes up the next morning, he notices that the fish has grown large and cannot suffice in the vessel. He then puts it in a tub of water, and the next morning it grows to the size of the tub. Shocked to see this manu puts matsya in a well, and next morning matsya grows as big as the well. Manu is shocked again; he puts him in the pond nearby, and sleeps again. Next morning matsya grows as big as the pond. Manu feels there is something fishy, ironically matsyas growth isn't stopping and has to be put into the river again. This time manu is careful; he observes this pattern and knows he has no option now if matsya grows as big as the river. He knows this is some trick of the gods, he folds his hands in wonder and requests god to show him what is that they are hinting him at.

Finally **Vishnu** appears out of the matsya, hence matsya being Vishnus first avatar. Vishnu says; now that you have uncovered the pattern of the ever growing desires in mans life, it is time you stop gathering knowledge and turn your heads up to the sky in faith and realise that no knowledge is sufficient for man to realise god, but when he gives up his race and surrenders to me, is when I appear to him. With this manu is finally fully self realised. Vishnu tells him that the day of the end of the world, called **pralaya** is near and he is the chosen one who will lend his hand and walk into the new life. Vishnu says he has prepared a boat and with him he needs to assemble the seven rishis called saptrishis, few selected animals, plants, and most importantly Vasuki-the serpent god with him and wait on the river shore for the boat to arrive. This is the same story countless novels, movies have been trying to tell us. Remember Neo from the matrix, he is the manu of that movie. He is the chosen one, and gods are trying to make him deserving of going into the next form, training him in all ways.

This is the story of all awakened men, this is why awakening exists in the midst of the great chaos of society. This is gods way of collecting his army, to see through the boat of life, training them rigorously and hitting them hard with nails and scorching heats of the cosmic game. When they do get awakened, a great desire opens up to speak out their truth, this is another natural way of god letting his power of creation, his power to collect his army through his finest creation, that is man himself. In general concepts this is how we learn the concept of multi level maketing. A top boss trains few managers, and then they train more, and a chain continues. Awakening being a very rare event requires a chain of events before one can uncover the great conflict of the cosmic game, to uncover his meatly desires, his crafty emotions and his never quenching cravings. This takes lifetimes, and the one who step into the boat, step with an ever absorbing desire to tell their story, most of them although fail in their first attempt. But they do not fail for eternity, they keep trying, they keep learning the fact that simply stating the truth is in no means a way of making people realise it too. The spiritual mastery is hence not their individual quest or their egoistic desire, but a way to bring about the purpose of god himself. They are serving him in their own ways but through his voice and his command.

The spiritual master fails and fails and fails, but doesn't give up, his quest is now to prepare a way for others to realise the greater truth. Hence religions were born in different parts of the world, in different eras, different prophets were born, different sadhus, enumorous saints. And people are bewildered to know why they are doing what they are doing. The answer is immaterial here, the work might seem illogical and uncanny on the surface but only they know what drives them.

The realization of the never ending desires is the last truth of the buddha or the manu, from where he starts his journey into researching what might bring man closer to the truth.

Bhagvad Geeta, Chapter 9, Verse 1

The Supreme Lord said: My dear Arjuna, because you are never envious of Me, I shall impart to you this most secret wisdom, knowing which you shall be relieved of the miseries of material existence.

Here krishna is giving away the truth to arjuna again in a vehicle, not a boat but a chariot this time and is training him throughout the course of the battle to become deserving of the truth and then he finally reveals to him his true nature. Not so to prove a point, but to make him ready to carry on with his game, for when the world closes its eyes, it can re open through the hands of Arjuna and his stories.

The understanding of the nodes is hence simply here another way of realising the conflict of the cosmic game, which if lived through one's own life would give him sufficient training through his earthly struggles to finally make him surrender to the lord himself. The understanding of the nodes is not simply a way to have a lavish house, a new mercedes and any sort of knowledge or power of the game that god provides man to play. This is simply living in the right direction from where the sound of the universe (Aum) becomes audible to man.

Bhagvad Geeta, <u>Chapter 9, Verse 3</u>

Those who are not faithful on the path of devotional service cannot attain Me, O conqueror of foes, but return to birth and death in this material world.

This is where Krishna says, that the way to realise me is through surrender and surrender alone. There is no other way. And one who does not realise me here and now will be born again in this struggle, as he has failed to grasp the word of mine through the struggles I gave him. He escaped, he dug a hole and went inside it. But how far can he hide, he will be born again and again in this material world till he finally surrenders to me.

And in the end when Krishna reveals his true opulence to arjuna, he says I will keep coming, again and again through you. Through your eyes I will shine and bring forth the heavens again when the universe closes and opens it eyes.

"Men go to far greater lengths to avoid what they fear than to obtain what they desire"

— Dan Brown

The Story Of Kacha
The Fulfillment Of Desires

Kacha was the son of Brihaspati (the teacher of the gods). In the everlasting ongoing battles between the gods and the demons, there was a definite reason why the gods were absolutely terrified of losing the battle. The reason was a special power or a special skill that Shukracharya, the teacher of the demons possessed.

The power called mritya-sanjivani (mritya meaning death and sanjivani means to bring back to life). Mritya-sanjivani was the yogic skill to bring back the dead to life. So every time the gods fought hard to kill a demon, he was brought back to life. And this way, howsoever great weapons the gods used, howsoever great strategies they made, it was of no use as Shukracharya always brought back his dead warriors to life after the battle. To this, Brihaspati approached Lord Brahma for a solution, Brahma said that u will be blessed with a son born with the desire to learn the art of mritya sanjivani. To this brihaspati said, but this is not possible as the skill can only be taught by Shukracharya and why will he ever want to teach this skill to my son. Brahma kept silent to this question and disappeared.

In due time, Shukracharya was born with a beautiful and handsome boy which he named Kacha. Kacha grew up between the battles of the gods and the demons and was relentless in learning the skill that would turn the tables on this great war. Kacha being a very attractive man tried to use his manly prowess to seduce Shukracharyas daughter Devayani in an attempt to become a disciple of Shukracharya. And when devayani did fall for him, he asked him to request his father to accept him as his disciple. The plan worked and Shukracharya very carefully accepted him as his disciple and kept him at a distance from his core inner yogic skiils, he made him do mineal jobs and kept him on the outskirts of the duties of the ashram.

In the meantime, the demons got to know about kacha and his disciplehood, afraid of directly questioning shukracharya, they themselves believe that kacha will surely become the reason for their fall, and hence start tracing kachas whereabouts in an attempt to get rid of him forever.

Kacha in his routine mineal jobs goes to the forest to collect wood and water everyday, the demons find him unarmed and helpless in such a situation and far away from Shukracharya to be helped. They quickly circle around him and kill him with a big club, kacha falls spot dead on the ground. The evening passes and devayani keeps waiting for kacha to return, devayani fills with anxiety and worry for his lover and starts looking for him in the forest. To her great shock she finds him on the ground bleeding from his head, no pulse is felt, no breath is heard. He is surely dead. Devayani cries out so hard that her weeps reach the ears and heart of Shukracharya. Shukracharya comes to the scene and assures his daughter that he will bring back kacha to life and she need not cry anymore. Shukracharya does what he promised, and kacha is brought back to life thorugh his powers of mritya-sanjivani.

The demons become angry at this, and the same killing is attempted again, and the same scene ensues, Devayani cries and shukracharya brings kacha back to life. The demons are puzzled now as to understand a way to finally kill kacha for eternity. This time when kacha goes to the forest, the demons not only kill him, but cut him into finely chopped pieces, almost making a powdery paste out of his bones and flesh. This powder could also be assembled and brought back to life by shukracharya so they mix this powder in shukracharyas wine and wait for him to drink it. Now the scene follows again, devayani cries but this time she does not find kachas body, Shukracharya uses his psychic vision to trace kacha and finds him inside his own stomach, now there is a problem he says. Shukracharya tells devayani if kacha is to be brought back to life he will come out blasting his stomach and killing him. So he asks his daughter to choose one among the two, his lover or his father. Devayani says that they both are equally beloved to her and cannot forsake one for the other. Shukracharya now is left with only one option but to teach kacha the mritya sanjivani mantra, addressing him inside his stomach. He recites the words to kacha inside his stomach and then recites it aloud himself bringing kacha blasting out of his stomach. Kacha tears off his stomach and comes out alive, killing shukracharya. Having learnt the mrityasanjivani mantra, kacha recites the mantra bringing shukracharya back to life and fulfilling the divine purpose of his incarnation.

In the fulfillment of ones desires, one need not be running and chasing his desires as kacha did. If kacha is observed closely, he only becomes aware of the fact about where the treasure of his life actually resides, he finds an intelligent way of being in the midst of the cave where his treasure lies. Coming to this cave had issues that were societal and were there since he was born, it was not easy to be in the company of Shukracharya, where his purpose resided. He found his tools of intelligence, his charm, his wits, his speaking abilities to come closer and closer to the spot where his treasure was. He never uttered a word of mritya-sanjivani in his entire life, yet the whole universe conspired to bring it to him, even though he had to die a thousand times in the pursuit of it. He did not shake, he did not surrender, never asking shukracharya directly for it, he kept his patience and in the end all the dots connected. His adversaries and his adversities all worked in turn not in killing him but if seen closely in bringing him towards his treasure. So when in life we are turned down by adversities, we must always remember to look closely and find out how the universe is conspiring in giving us exactly what we need and not become a barrier in its process. We must keep here in the domain of this book a sharp focus in keeping in tune with our north node and not become fearful in the way of its fulfillment. The way of the north node is definitely scary, coz it is yet unknown. It brings a great fear in the heart of the individual as to what will people say if I start behaving out of tune with my nature, will I be ever accepted this way, but this is exactly the trick. When we do start to live by it, then not only people accept but accept and appreciate us with open arms. We become the centre around which the universe itself revolves, and true fulfillment and unparalleled bliss follows such a kind of a beautifully stable life.

Planets And Signs Descriptions And Generalisations

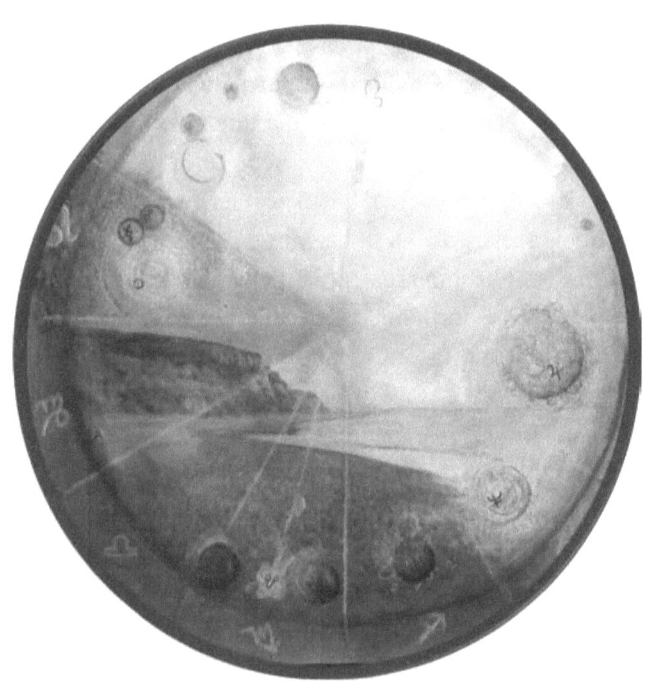

Astrology studies the relationship between the movement of bodies and planets in the firmament and the inner and outer life of man. Astrology is also perceived by many as an occult science. It is based on the idea of reality as controlled by the impersonal will of the Absolute - the root cause of the entire manifested world - and the concept of reincarnation, according to which each person has an immortal soul, and, being consistently embodied in different conditions, seeks to gain a certain experience, to get free from the shackles of her shells and dissolve in the Absolute that originally gave birth to it.

Astrology considers the movement of planets from a geocentric point of view; in addition, it (mainly, but always in this course) is limited to considering the ecliptic plane, that is, the plane in which the Earth's orbit is located. Constellations lying in the plane of the ecliptic are called zodiacal: Aries, Taurus, Gemini, Cancer, Leo, Virgo, Libra, Scorpio, Sagittarius, Capricorn, Aquarius, Pisces. Since the Sun is in the plane of the ecliptic, it, from the point of view of the Earth, at each moment in time is in a certain zodiac constellation. The remaining planets (except the Moon and Pluto) rotate in planes close to the ecliptic; their position in the zodiac is calculated by first projecting on the ecliptic.

In a typical western astrological chart there are majorly three defined terms that need to be understood in their intrinsic nature to relate them to the self and thereby to individual life forms.

These terms are: **1. Planets 2. Houses 3. Signs**

Let us understand these three terms as part of a theatrical play. Imagining this as a play of human life, where houses are decorations (spheres of life), planets are actors, and signs are styles of performance, and the events of the play are played out in transit of planets from one house to another.

PLANETS OF ASTROLOGY

Planets can also be simply seen as they are taught to us in primary school being all the planetary bodies surrounding us assuming we are standing on earth at a particular position marked by the latitude and longitude of that place. Hence, what we have here are 8 planets of the solar system namely mercury, venus, mars, Jupiter, Saturn, Uranus, neptune, Pluto. And then we have the influence of the sun and moon as well on the earth. So we have here typically 10 planetary bodies each moving through space in their own orbits, hence creating different permutations and combinations of energy forces on the point of reference of us on the earth.

MERCURY

Rules Gemini, is in detriment in Sagittarius, is exalted in Aquarius and falls in Leo.

Mercury is responsible for the rational unemotional thinking and speech. However thinking itself is to a big extent an unconscious and intuitive process so it is not possible to name only one planet that controls thinking in humans. Mercury is responsible for the expression of thought in speech, that is, for the final part of the thinking process.

Mercury is also responsible for all kinds of human contacts, excluding their emotional part, that is, negotiations, transactions, transmission of information and (together with Mars) for sports, especially those with the ball.

Most common ways to grasp the principle of Mercury: analysis, intelligence, interactions, contacts, short trips

Weak Mercury makes one's speech unclear - native might be not able to formulate his own thoughts and bring them to the others. Also weak unmastered Mercury may give us an intriguer, a prudent but not wise person.

Strong Mercury makes one's speech precise and clear, eases the thinking process and finally leads one to the wisdom.

VENUS

Rules Libra and Taurus, is in detriment in Scorpio, is exalted in Pisces and falls in Virgo.

Just like Moon, Venus is carrying a strong feminine energy. But unlike Moon (which represents the principle of adaptive perception at the biological level), Venus is dealing with the social levels of our being. Venus also determines the aesthetic features of one's perception of his environment (most often than not related to the native's social circle) and is directly related to love in all its manifestations.

Harmony and beauty that undoubtedly exist in any phenomena and any situation can be seen only by tuning in to it and disconnecting attention from oneself; God can be found anywhere, but one has to be able to see.

Therefore native's perception has to be not only biological (Moon), but also social (Venus). Venus will let native not only to see beauty and harmony in the world around him, but also to radiate it becoming a source of attraction. This gentle force is just as real and often no less effective than a direct pressure (often provided by Sun or Mars).

Most common ways to grasp the principle of Venus: Desires (as in wishes), feelings, love, art, beauty, harmony, tendency to balance and enjoy.

Weak Venus brings difficulties in social interactions, bad or way too kinky taste. Native may seem untactful, ugly.

Strong Venus gives a very good natured person, strongly connected to the world through his well developed programs of perceiving its harmony (God's law).

MARS

Rules Aries ans Scorpio, is in detriment in Libra, is exalted in Capricorn and falls in Cancer.

Mars in one's chart is responsible for activation of energies. Here we must think not only the energies that are manifesting themselves externally, but also those manifesting within - aggressive instincts (including active part of sexual instinct).

In traditional astrology Mars was perceived as malefic planet causing troubles to the native. However people of the past were most like in lack of control over their impulsive behavior so more often than not aggressiveness (internal and external) was manifested quite directly. In reality Mars gives native a lot of creative energy and the joy of physical manifestation (joy of labor if work is perceived as interesting, joy of participating in sports, dancing etc) and generally connects native to the physical world in a very open and active manner.

Situations ruled by Mars or those when Mars is active are easily determined - native will necessarily be affected directly either by physical forces (for example punched in the face) or by inner forces (native's own instincts and desires).

Most common ways to grasp the principle of Mars: action, willpower, planet of warriors (soldiers), direct fights and confrontations.

Strong Mars gives determination and bravery (sometimes bordering with recklessness), strong instincts. In general Mars is enhancing all characteristics of the sign where it resides.

Weak Mars gives clumsiness, difficulties in physical manifestations. In water signs Mars may give capriciousness (but not in Scorpio as in this sign Mars is exceptionally strong).

PLUTO

Rules Scorpio, is in detriment in Taurus, is exalted in Leo and falls in Aquarius.

The very first thing we need to know about Pluto - this planet doesn't manifest in undeveloped individuals. Pluto is one of the so-called "highest planets" (other two are Uranus and Neptune). Also Pluto is often called "higher Mars". It is in a sleeping state in the individual who doesn't show any signs of spiritual awakening and the more awakened and aware native becomes - the more Pluto manifestations will be observed.

Pluto is an embodiment of power in all possible senses of this word. Pluto controls destinies of crowds as well as he manages the deepest programs of human subconscious, which are very rarely obvious, but nevertheless they constantly subtly affect native's life, externally and internally.

Most common ways to grasp the principle of Pluto: power, collective will, transformation, forces of nature, deep powerful flows of anything.

We do not speak here of weak Pluto as it is virtually impossible. Pluto in one's chart can only be not weak but unmanifested.

Manifested Pluto is always strong and getting stronger in case native is growing spiritually. Pluto puts native through many hard challenges and if one passes the test - gives powers to control others and to have perfect clarity of vision (in all possible meanings of this word).

SUN

Rules Leo, is in detriment in Aquarius, is exalted in Aries and falls in Libra.

In traditional astrology Sun is considered to be the most important planet in the chart. Indeed it has a large influence on one's personality. However from my personal practice and experience I can see that Sun being in a certain zodiac sign is mainly manifesting native's mask. The one that he wears in front of others. His most favorite mask. His role that is played by him with most ease.

Sun is something one thinks of himself, of his public representations, of his decisions (mostly again - in the eyes of society, others).

No wonder it is proclaimed as most important planet of the chart - it is indeed easy to work with simply because Sun is always on the surface and can be understood much easier than some other planets.

Most common ways to grasp the principle of Sun - self identification, conscious position in life, will, personal initiatives, life situations that force native to take action, native's way to present himself to others.

Strong Sun will let native to express himself quite easily. Such native is not easily influenced by others or by events of his life.

Weak Sun will make one more agreeable but less able to self express.

MOON

Rules Cancer, is in detriment in Capricorn, is exalted in Taurus and falls in Scorpio (it is the only case when the fallen planet doesn't loose it's power as Scorpio itself is a very powerful sign so Moon in Scorpio will be in it's full powers.

Traditionally Moon is representing the subconscious as a whole. Moon is responsible for adaptation and reflex reactions. When a person behaves without hesitation and in accordance with well-established (often in childhood) norms and rules it will be almost always according to the Moon's position in sign. When a person speaks in cliches, hears only what he has long been well aware of - this is also the Moon. Moon is a symbol of mother, it shows the strength, role and type of maternal influence in a person's childhood, as well as the role of the feminine in adulthood. For a man, Moon shows the type of woman who is likely to be his wife and, in any case, the image that he will impose on her. In a woman's chart Moon shows the features of her own feminine principle and the ways of its realization.

Most common ways to grasp the principle of Moon - Perception, emotions, habitual reactions, subconscious reactions, adaptation, socially established patterns of behavior that are written into subconscious structures.

Strong Moon gives us a very emotional native, often compassionate, often "trusting his heart more than his head", very caring maternal figure (even if it's a man we are talking about). With strong Moon native himself feels at peace more often than not.

Weak Moon will give us native who appears to be not very emotional, more rational. May have trust issues. Weak Moon often makes one restless and insecure.

URANUS

Rules Aquarius, is in detriment in Leo, is exalted in Scorpio and falls in Taurus.

Uranus can be described as a friendly eccentric who's main job in human life is to bring the most new, the most progressive and the most unconventional phenomena. Any sphere of native's life that is affected by Uranus will be the source of unexpected and (most likely) misunderstood actions, ideas and events.

Uranus is a revolutionary who brings ideas to the forms (physical and mental ones) that are never completely ready. Energy of this planet is always strong and it always enters native's life suddenly - as a sudden catastrophe or a sudden genius insight (depending on the level of mastery).

Most common ways to grasp the principle of Uranus: unpredictability, reformations, eccentricity, futuristic mindset.

Weak (here we mean low level of mastery) Uranus in one's chart is connected with mental illnesses, sudden inappropriate reactions. In some cases energy of this planet may cause electric shocks, nervous breakdowns or simply dysfunction of house electric appliances (have you ever met someone who enters your house and all your light bulbs go off? this is the case).

Strong Uranus (well mastered by native) brings changes of the highest order. This is quite possible that energies of Uranus are connected to one's enlightenment.

This is Podvodny's quote (not really for the book maybe, but for you personally):

For almost the entire second half of the 20th century, from 1951 to 1991, the Chiron - Uranus opposition stands in the sky, which gives an accelerated expansion of consciousness, a strong (sometimes too strong) channel of communication between the higher and lower "self", a strong desire for spiritual progress, not realized fully for various reasons, including due to the low emotional and spiritual culture and the almost zero level of occult literacy in the Western world. When this aspect is active in native's chart, life becomes interesting, restless, and at times there is a feeling that fate is forcing him to become a saint [I suspect here he means "enlightened"].

NEPTUNE

Rules Pisces, is in detriment in Virgo, is exalted in Cancer and falls in Capricorn.

Neptune is a ruler of ecstatic states therefore this planet is connected to hypnotism, hallucinations, inspiration, meditation practices. Neptune gives native a feeling of divine order in all matters of the house where it is situated. However if not mastered properly it may easily make native delusional, misguided, self fooled.

Neptune is a cosmic magic maker. But it largely depends on how it's principles are mastered: it may give native an opportunity to have the most profound insights in the framework of the house or (in case Neptune's energies are used on a very low level) become nothing but a cheap trick or a trap (along with the highest art Neptune rules also drug addicts and alcoholics).

Most common ways to grasp the principle of Neptune: deep unconscious processes, faith, fantasies, hallucinations, ideals, pure love, lies.

Weak Neptune (low level of mastery) is pushing native into the spiderweb of lies, illusions and fake insights.

Strong Neptune is representing divine love in it's highest possible form. Native with strong Neptune is attracting other people like a magnet. His interactions are full of pure unconditional love from both sides. His creative abilities are beyond imaginable.

JUPITER

Rules Sagittarius and Pisces, is in detriment in Gemini, is exalted in Cancer and falls in Capricorn.

In traditional astrology Jupiter is believed to be a benefactor giving gifts and expanding one's possibilities. In some cases indeed Jupiter is acting as a guardian angel providing native with kind attitude, good mood, joyfulness, feeling of trust and love for people.

However the real job of Jupiter in one's chart is not just blindly giving gifts regardless of how well deserved (or undeserved at all) they are. What he really does? He is showing where (in what areas of existence) native will have more or less easy ways to achieve some considerable level of success. To show doesn't mean to give. The trick here is that native can clearly see the opportunity but (as it is programmed in his structure) he may feel that the desirable result is already his. So being fooled by Jupiter's optimistic shine native feels that the prize is already in his hands and refuses to work for it.

The most common ways to grasp principle of Jupiter: development, community values, wealth, law, social goals, expansion, wisdom in terms of broad mind.

Strong Jupiter makes native optimistic, good natured kind and merry person. May give love for traveling and knowledge.

Weak Jupiter gives excessive pride, makes native blind to the challenges of reality, replaces true knowledge with cliches.

SATURN

Rules Capricorn and Aquarius, is in detriment in Cancer and Leo, is exalted in Libra and falls in Aries.

Most traditional astrologers believe Saturn to be a malefic planet (or at least very difficult to deal with). Indeed demands of Saturn in one's chart are quite imperative and rarely easy to fulfill. This is because he works with those patterns of our lives where we are supposed to be deprived of our freedom in order to attain our goals. Rare native will feel grateful in this situation.

However when one masters principles of Saturn in his chart he becomes wiser, he learns to see and operate his limitations, to perform in situations where his personal will has to be ignored for the grater good.

Saturn is teaching discipline. He let us to study how to live in limited environment where we only have the very necessary basics to survive. Placement of Saturn will show the wound we are born with and in course of life we study how to heal it so by the end there will be only a scar left to remind us of the journey.

The most common ways to grasp principle of Saturn: limitations, control, discipline, time, age, wisdom.

Strong Saturn gives native wisdom to detect the most difficult parts of his path and endurance to pass them with dignity and minimal losses.

Weak Saturn gives subconscious fears, general fear of living and dying. Inability to make difficult decisions, to calculate possible outcomes, to gain knowledge from traumatic situations.

Elaboration Of The Nodes The Study Of Human Nodular Evolution

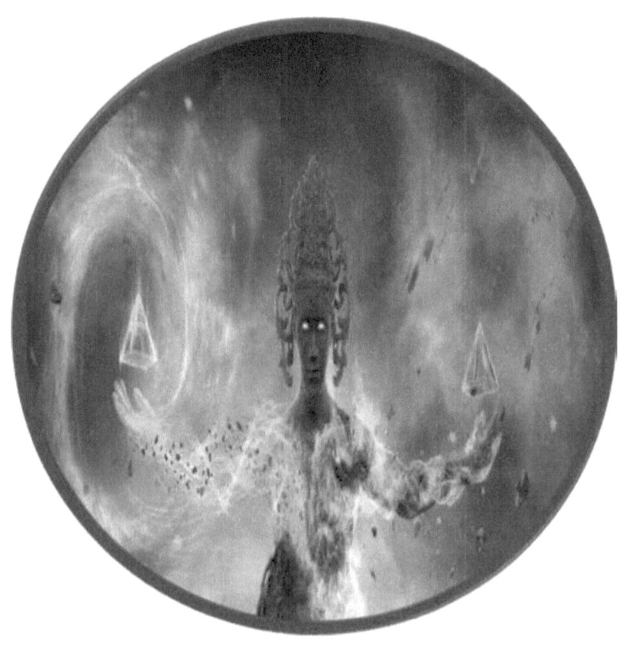

The nodes of the moon are not as sensitive points of the horoscope as the planets. They are not visible in the firmament, do not represent, like the planets of principles, and are not sources of energy. Their role is more likely to be mediating: they represent features of the dynamics of human development: his personal evolution and his participation in the evolution of the world. More precisely, the nodes of the Moon characterize the diachronic aspect of the inclusion of man in the processes of evolution of the inner and outer world, that is, his dependence on the inner experience of his soul and the past of his people and his attitude to this past, as well as trends in the future development of both.

Any development is in the balance of the past and the future; if this balance is violated towards the future, a person burns bridges too quickly behind him and finds himself in a vacuum, losing his foundation and direction of further movement; if the balance is disturbed in the direction of the past, then development stops and stamping on the ground, fermentation, and then decay of stagnation begin.

The nodes of the moon always mean specific circumstances, although less certain than at home. The passage of time and external and internal development is often invisible to consciousness, but is always recorded by the subconscious. And regarding each event and phenomenon, the question arises before him: how to relate to this? As an old, familiar, familiar one, which should be placed in familiar schemes, or as a new one, which requires accepting oneself as such and creating special schemes or a place in classifications over time.

The first process is controlled by the Southern node of the moon, the second - by the North. The same problem arises in a person when included in social life. Each external event can be considered as a manifestation of the established course of the life of society, or you can see in it something fundamentally new, which only today enters into social life and has never been seen before. Human perception and reactions to these types of social phenomena are completely different and are also determined by the position in the map, respectively, of the southern and northern nodes of the moon.

The development of the nodes of the Moon goes along those lines: the study of the Southern node, the Northern node and the establishment of a balance between them. In general, the North and South nodes are better viewed not separately, but as two faces of the same object; this is manifested, for example, in the fact that they always seem to be aspected (for example, they are necessarily both harmonious or amazed).

The nodes of the moon play a very large role in human life. Depending on the level of their study and the greater or lesser accentuation of one of them, there is the daily life of a person and his everyday worldview, for example, he lives yesterday, today or tomorrow; in addition, with the defeat of the major planets (the Sun and the Moon) or simply at a low level of elaboration of the map, a person often realizes himself, emphasizing the nodes that can give him work and shelter without affecting his central mental structures: it will be life without signs of elaboration, the framework of social reality, where a person represents a role, for which he is paid moderate money, but does not require anything else.

The development of each of the nodes follows two main lines: a more detailed and deep vision of the corresponding phenomena and the correlation of the external and internal values of this node, that is, the problems of the development of society and man himself. Below are four levels of node development, which should be taken as indicative, since their development is often uneven, and it may well turn out that a person, for example, has the South node at the fourth level of development, and the North at the second, and what is the level the elaboration of their balance can be said only by studying the life of a given person.

At the first level of elaboration of nodes, the person's consciousness and subconscious mind are fully coordinated with social ones, and he is a retrograde together with everyone, and he welcomes progressive ideas, especially when they promise quick enrichment, also with everyone. At this level it is completely useless to discuss with a person issues related to the department of nodes, that is, what is and what is not new and how to relate to it; he, depending on the mutual accentuation and aspects of the nodes, may be more or less friendly towards the past and the future, but his views are unshakable, and he cannot (and does not want) change them. It should be emphasized that the South Node determines a person's attitude to the past not in itself, but in the form presented in the present, that is, to tradition, established attitudes, rites, ways of behavior in stereotypical situations, etc. Accordingly, the Northern Node determines the attitude of a person not to the distant future, but to those fragments that not only have already materialized in the present, but have received social recognition, that is, they have become a fact of public life

At the first level of elaboration of knots, a person is characterized by an extremely superficial, although dogmatic, attitude towards tradition. He knows her firsthand and formally adopted several rules that have become dogmas for him, "because our grandfathers lived like that, and they were smarter than us." When required, he forgets both tradition and smart grandfathers, and does as he currently needs and is comfortable, and the feeling of contradiction in his words and actions does not reach his consciousness, either from within or from attempts to clarify from the outside. A typical attitude towards new trends is superficially skeptical, with a touch of contempt ("that they can understand") or arrogant perplexity ("I don't understand what is good in this, but since I don't understand, it means nothing"), or, in in rare cases, superficially encouraging with an anticipation of easy money ("let's try, and if that works out, we'll warm our hands together").

The development of the inner world at this level is almost without the participation of consciousness and mainly along the line of accumulation of impressions and experiences; comprehension of past experience and conscious adaptation to new phenomena of inner life does not occur, they meet with the same distrust or narrow self-interest as news of external social life. The past, present and future of external (and internal) life are not connected by a person into a single whole and their mutual influence on each other is not even realized. The external and internal world appear completely static and chaotic.

For this level of elaboration of nodes, hard-dogmatic upbringing of children is characteristic, which, according to a person's thought, must exactly correspond to the social norm, on the one hand, and achieve all that he has not achieved, on the other; Thus, parental frustrations are projected onto children, which ensures the continuity of generations, the connection of times and the balance of nodes at the first level of their development.

At the second level of elaboration of nodes, a person is sometimes already able to form a point of view on certain phenomena of the present in their connection with the past and future, not reduced to a social stamp. However, here the development is proceeding more likely not along the path of overcoming it, but along the path of deepening into the tradition, its detailed study and comprehension; The Northern Node is being worked out, respectively, by a more careful examination of new social phenomena, by searching for their roots and problems, which they have echoed. At this level, a person as a whole still follows the social subconscious, but is already beginning to divide the tradition into its obsolete, inert part and a solid foundation, which is absolutely necessary, but in itself insufficient and needs additional construction measures. With regard to new social trends, he departs from a flat-pragmatic view and admits that he may not understand something in the ideas of the younger generation, which are not all rubbish and rubbish, and that he needs to grow inwardly to understand them. This attitude is much more constructive, and a person adapts to those new phenomena of social life that are completely ignored by people at the first level of elaboration of nodes or hit them like a butt on the head.

As for the dynamics of the inner world, at this level of elaboration of nodes, a person in principle recognizes the possibility and even the need for internal development, but is still completely unable to manage it; at best, he partially monitors it, although he hardly believes that it is really changing, even when it is already obvious to his whole environment. Here, the idea of internal development corresponds to the Saturn-Jupiterian ideas, that is, the development of internal discipline and concentration of attention (South Node) and the expansion of spheres of interests and activities (North Node), and thus is still quite consistent with social norms. However, the idea of reconciling the person's internal development with the external development of society (the way a person sees him) has not yet come to mind, just like the idea of the interconnection of stability and variability in the evolutionary development of man and society as a whole is still completely abstract, he can't practically attach it yet. The outer and inner world seems, in theory, developing, but people still cannot see their development as a whole, and not through the evolution of small fragments, and although they recognize the connection of times, they also feel it very fragmentarily and not always.

At this level of node development, parents allow certain liberties in the upbringing of children, not insisting on their exact compliance with the standard and assuming that they themselves (when they become adults) can and should determine their fate; at the same time, their fate is conceived nevertheless mainly within the social framework and most often within the parental social layer (or the next in level). The balance of nodes at this level is symbolized by the vision in children of their own character traits in their youth and the establishment of balanced relations with their parents.

At the third level of elaboration of nodes, a person significantly departs from the social cliches of perceiving tradition and new social trends. He has his own views on both, and may consider it rational in the tradition that in his environment is considered unconditionally positive and necessary; equally, he can accept new trends that are inaccessible and categorically rejected by most contemporaries. However, it is more significant that at this level of elaboration of nodes an individual attitude is formed to all current phenomena of social life, which are now divided into ordinary and new categories not in strict accordance with the standards of public consciousness and subconsciousness, but on the basis of personal intuition. This means that a person is connected to a social egregor, at first as a pure observer, monitoring the dynamics of the development of society. This is the level of talented publicists, fashionable writers with noisy but mercenary fame, sometimes major public figures. These people see many connections between past, present and future, and the latter rarely catches them by surprise.

In the field of inner life, the third level of elaboration of nodes means that a person already sees quite well the trends in its development. He understands which subconscious programs are obsolete and which reappearing are relevant for the future and, to some extent, learn to manage interaction with the rest of the psyche.

At this level, a circumstance that previously was completely imperceptible is manifested: the connection between the difficulties of personal and social development, at least in the form in which they appear to this person. In order to understand one, it often turns out to be useful to understand the other, and a person begins to realize the meaning of the principle of duality of his external and internal world on a very important aspect: the evolution of both. Now he sees significant connections connecting the past, present and future of the external world and his soul with through threads, which immediately makes meaningful both its internal development and life in the external world; also a meaningful and almost concrete occupation is the search for one's place in the evolutionary process.

At this level, a person looks at children as close, but still independent souls entrusted with his upbringing, and their freedom in choosing fate seems to him natural and, moreover, their inherent affiliation; nevertheless, if their ethics is very different from the parent, the person will experience and doubt the quality of their education. At this level, a person sees his upbringing function equally as social and spiritual, and the balance of nodes is symbolized by the transfer of those and other aspirations of a higher order from parents to children.

At the fourth level of elaboration of nodes, a person sees social karma well, and the inner meaning of processes and phenomena occurring in society is open to him. These are national prophets and spiritual teachers, in rare (at least in the era of Pisces) cases - major religious, social and political figures. At this level, a person can influence the development of social processes, not only by visible external actions, but also by direct work in the egregor. The location of the nodes in the night and day hemispheres will show where it is more convenient for him to work externally, and where - directly through the egregor. The southern node symbolizes a tradition that must be partially overcome, and partially used, being able to lean on it; The northern node symbolizes new trends, in which it is also necessary to select a rational grain and carefully germinate it, separating it from the chaff. Both of these can be done only with attention, understanding not only the main course of karma, but also the huge amount of social foam covering it from above, which is possible only at the following levels of elaboration of nodes; it is important, however, to understand that this is partially possible at the fourth and even lower levels of their elaboration, but it requires a complete rejection of personal and group interest and great internal honesty, because social leads in the subconscious mind are much thinner than leads of the ego, and therefore their distortions can go unnoticed longer. Any person is a child of his time and social layer, and abandoning this means going out into the airless space, where it is very difficult to adapt.

In the field of inner life, at the fourth level of elaboration of nodes, qualitative changes occur with a person. He begins to feel the experience of previous incarnations of his soul; sometimes specific memories come to him. He can generally foresee his future, sometimes with great accuracy. The coherence and unity of fate is obvious to him, although a sense of complete harmony of the world has not yet been achieved. At this level, the need for internal work for external success is obvious, as is the relationship between internal and social problems; moreover, a person can sometimes solve the latter by successfully working on the former.

In raising children at this level, the main emphasis a person makes is to give their soul the most favorable opportunities for manifestation. Outwardly, this may look quite ordinary (or maybe not), but children will feel great the lack of internal pressure from their parents, and their creative abilities will be above average. At this level, a person can see the evolutionary meaning of small things in the life of a child and regulate his behavior with the help of minor, purely external restrictions. Here, the balance of nodes is symbolized by the transfer to children of a common spiritual aspiration, regardless of the differences in their social reality from their parent.

The situation of nodes is typical for discussing the problems of social development in the entire existing range - from the conversation of two elderly women about the degradation of the younger generation in comparison with the long past time of their youth to the polemic in the press about the right to exist another dance style. Many methods of social pastime are associated with the frank and unscrupulous exploitation of the lunar nodes: these are talks about raising children and fashion in the female circle and discussing political news and possible prospects for male presidential candidates; this also includes all kinds of memories of the good old days, morals and customs, and assessments of the present by the criteria of the past, as well as a discussion of the possible future in the strong positions of the present.

The situations of the lower octave nodes are usually unbalanced, that is, one of the nodes is accented stronger than the other. This leads to the fact that the discussion is completely useless and plays the role of exclusively spending time, which is not at all harmless, since the very idea of developing a society or, at least, participation of a given person in it is profane. On the other hand, there are practically no situations of a purely Southern and a purely Northern node, since the theme of another node will surely sound like a background that is easy to sense.

The global situation of nodes is, for example, the adoption by the people of a religion new to it or the introduction of a foreign culture, when many old rites and forms of social behavior are filled with new content. Depending on the level of the balance of nodes, such situations can go more or less harmoniously or, conversely, destructively.

The situation of nodes in a person's internal development usually arises with an emphasis on one of them: either the inert and inert part of the psyche slows down a person's development, or new programs are too energetically introduced into the subconscious, for which it is not yet ready. In both cases, the task of man is to find a balance of nodes and not to sacrifice the ruthlessly old for the sake of the new or vice versa.

The nodes in the map are usually aspected in a similar way: if the planet is squared to one of them, then to the other too, and the trine to the North node is accompanied by a sextile of the same planet to the South. An exception is the aspect of the connection, which gives the fundamental possibility of strengthening one node compared to another: the node in connection with the planet, and even more so, with several, is emphasized in the map stronger than the opposite.

A person with an emphasis on the South Node is tradition-oriented. He is happy to look for traces of the past in the present, and when working out the Southern Knot, he sometimes finds something that was unknown to anyone, or draws attention to what is escaping from the others. Karmically, this person is called to guard the foundations, to be responsible for the foundation of an ever-growing social building. At a low level of elaboration, and especially with the defeat of nodes, it is a retrograde and desperate conservative, blindly believing everything that was before, and rejecting the new only because it is new. The study here provides a deep insight into the problems of the present as arising from the past and not only a vision of the foundation of the tradition, but also the ability to putty minor cracks in it, greatly increasing its reliability without major repairs. It should be added that these actions are carried out by the people of the South Node, following the lateral vision of the trends in the future development of society, which gives it a general orientation.

In inner life, a person with an emphasis on the South Node is inclined to believe that he is fundamentally, in the main, quite good and needs, in extreme cases, only the most minor improvements. At a low level, he is also skeptical of the idea of adapting his psyche to any new conditions, believing that all this pampering is nothing to talk about (that is, nothing really happened to him and cannot happen). He is well adapted to himself, and can firmly lean on himself, which provides the basis for development, but in his absence leads to ossification and degradation of the personality.

A person with an accent of the Northern Node will be more interested in new and, as he believes, promising social movements than in traditions. In a democratic society, it can often be seen at a demonstration, in a totalitarian society - the fig that he holds in his pocket will be larger than that of others.

However, one should distinguish the person of the Northern Node from the person of Aquarius: the first does not go beyond the social framework, while the second with great difficulty fits himself there at least partially. At a low level, the Northern Node person is too fashionable and superficially evaluates social news, welcoming them on the principle of freshness, and not on the merits of the trends that they reflect. During study, a person learns to better see the present and, penetratingly evaluating the sprouts of the future, helps them to develop, taking into account the peculiarities of their root system, which should grow into the present and strengthen in the deeper layers of the past, which he also observes with the corner of his eye.

In the inner life, a person of the Northern Node always strives for somewhere, not always understanding where and why. He often does not suit himself, or rather, he is boring and demands new things - new friends, impressions, changes in professions and hobbies. At a higher level of self-consciousness, he constantly strives to develop new qualities in himself, to master new programs of the subconscious and new mental reality, at first having a poor idea of how it will fit into the old and what will result from this. Further elaboration gives wisdom in these matters and the ability not to rush things, but this is given with difficulty, and the idea of the need for refinement and partial correction of old subconscious programs, in particular, habits, skills, systems of world views, etc. it remains unpleasant for a very long time, since it is always easier for a person of the Northern Node to throw it away than to fix it.

Strong nodes give a person who needs to live in the midst of life. Neither the past nor the future haunts him: he really likes the past in the present, but at the same time it is clearly outdated in places and requires a decisive replacement; future trends are also very attractive, and they need to be widely disseminated as soon as possible. At a low level, such a person profane the idea of social development completely; looking at it, it becomes quite obvious that this development is possible in the direction of more or less rapid degradation, because from the tradition it takes the most flat and reactionary part, and from new ideas it makes something either completely fantastic and unreal or, conversely, well recognizable, from the recent past, the very one in it that I want to bury and forget forever.

The study gives a deeper insight into the essence of what is happening in society, and then the idea of the need to find a synthesis of tradition and new trends and indicate concrete ways of development of society takes shape in the human mind, which, in fact, is the karmic program of nodes.

In inner life, a person with strong nodes will experience constant impulses of development; depending on the mutual accentuation of the nodes and their aspects, it will occur with emphasis on an established psychic reality or on the development of new subconscious programs, and more or less harmoniously, but a person must necessarily change (another thing is that he can profane his development, especially with harmonious nodes). Directions of development will show the houses where the nodes are, and their aspects; it should be borne in mind that the internal development is half at the expense of the South Node, when the achieved is conceptualized and finalized and its mental debris is cleaned and removed. Strong knots at a low level of elaboration give a terrible inner fuss, a person constantly rushes somewhere, sometimes strives to forge himself completely anew, destroying everything that is at the moment, then, on the contrary, completely rejects all innovations and focuses exclusively on the idea of thorough development and cultivating existing skills and abilities.

Unworked strong knots give complexes and frustrations of a very difficult kind - disbelief in oneself, the possibility of one's development and self-realization, which is projected outward and gives social nihilism and denial of the possibility of social development, despite the fact that a person can really work in areas related to social problems and development of society.

High demands on their own children, as well as attention to youth issues.

Weak nodes give a person who has little interest in social dynamics. The fashion of the younger generation does not cause him delight, but he will not boil with indignation when he hears a popular motive among young people. This provision gives non-inclusion in development by force, but does not mean stagnation: a person can both comprehend the development of the society around him and develop himself - there are no special obstacles in this, but there are no incentives to this, as with strong, and especially affected nodes.

The lack of elaboration of nodes, as well as the lack of elaboration of a weak Saturn, leads, however, to dire consequences: at some point, a person realizes that he is hopelessly behind in his development and has become ossified mentally, and is not able to rely on his existing subconscious programs, which have become very tough and largely primitive, nor start mastering new ones. On the other hand, the study of weak nodes is very promising, because it allows you to direct internal development along the path that will be chosen by the person himself, without peremptory pressure of external or internal circumstances, which is typical for strong nodes. In the field of social perception and interaction with the development of society, weak nodes mean the karma of the observer, and elaboration involves not so much balanced participation in the development of society as impartial observation of it with an increasing level of concentration. Here, the study provides a high level of understanding of development processes and a small (apparently) possibility of direct participation in them, which greatly distresses a person; and only at a high level of evolutionary development does he realize that his main function in the world is attention and understanding, and not an action that is always secondary.

The harmonious South Node provides an opportunity for a deep vision of the role of tradition in the modern life of society and a great love for it. This person can be a lover of antiquity in any form: to collect ancient chandeliers or books, to know in spite of the historical places of his city or to study recipes of ancient cuisine, to revive the rites and customs of his ancestors in his life, etc. For all this, he will have great taste and abilities, and he can go into such activities headlong, completely plunging into his beloved world and forgetting about everything else, but most importantly - about the laws of development. The dope of the past, especially perceived with nostalgic sweetness, can be stronger than opium and even heroin, and absorbs a weak person as a whole.

The vain promising Sextiles of the North Node invite him to pay attention to the problems of the development of the present and devote at least a small part of his time and attention - a person most often remains deaf to calls: the trins of the South Node give a very great inner passivity, a sense of the unnecessary development, in any case, of the application special efforts, because (it seems to man) everything should happen by itself, on time, harmoniously and beautifully, and if for the sake of something it is necessary to kill, God will manage with him, and so. This is one of the most difficult to overcome the situation, since oblique and obsolete subconscious programs are endowed with very great inertia, which can be overcome only by exertion of all forces, no matter what harmonious laziness says about this. Trin is an aspect of self-deception, when a square is seen as a beautiful oval with a rose on the edge. Here, the study provides great opportunities for development (internal and external) and harmonious participation in social life, when a person teaches others to see and respect the tradition in its living part and move forward on its basis, and not in empty space. Good for progressive priests of the official church and professors of central universities.

The harmonious North Node gives a person who bathes in new trends and progressive ideas; for him they are no worse than a drug. He does not want to think about the difficulties of implementation and the real constructiveness of these ideas and trends: he likes them for who they are. Without elaboration, this leads to a gradual devaluation of ideas and shredding of the person himself, since you can be inspired and inspired by other phantoms for a limited time. The trins of the North Node make the future evidently beautiful and equally inevitable, and it seems that nothing needs to be done but to greet him joyfully. Sextiles to the South Node show the directions of grounding: areas where you need to look for the roots and traditions, connecting with which the sprouts of the future, you can get a full and viable plant. But sextiles need to be realized somehow, they provide potential opportunities, and trines provide luck and ready-made opportunities, and the temptation of decisive preference of the Northern node to the Southern one may turn out to be strong, and this leads to a separation from reality and pure fantasy.

In inner life, a harmonious North Node means excellent ability to adapt to any new conditions, in particular, at a low level - a rubber conscience: a person can justify himself in any position. At the same time, adaptation of new programs of the subconscious to your psyche requires some work and attention to its existing state and dynamics, which is hinted at by the Sextile to the South Node; in the absence of their elaboration, it seems to a person that he has learned a new one, but in reality it strongly resembles a dry layered cake, which, with light pressure from above, becomes like a hedgehog: the old and the new lie in layers, do not interact and do not mix, so that the synthesis of the whole does not occur.

Two extreme cases of harmonious nodes were analyzed above: the first - when all the trines go to the South node, and the second - when to the North. In the intermediate case, when part of the planets in the map forms trines to the South, and part to the North, and there are no squares to the nodes, we can say that the nodes are approximately equally harmonious. This, however, does not at all remove the problems of the relationship of the trin of a given planet to one of the nodes to its sextile to another; the elaboration of these aspects proceeds in parallel, in accordance with the descriptions given above, related to the areas controlled by this planet, and in the absence of elaboration, a person will be naively retrograde in some areas and so superficially progressive in others, in accordance with the aspects of the nodes.

The affected nodes give a person who is difficult to look at the development of the surrounding society: the traditions of the past do not suit him, seem silly, dogmatic, long outdated or unnecessary, and the trends for the new seem not to be a way out of this situation, but a mockery of common sense (Mercury square to the nodes), aesthetic feeling (square of Venus) or existence (square of the Moon). At the same time, problems of the development of society touch a person; he cannot manage to hide from them so easily; he is constantly involved in some kind of social currents, into which he energetically engages and from which he is equally energetically torn away, to the mutual displeasure of the parties. Without elaboration, this person can become a complete social nihilist, perverting and denying both tradition and all progressive trends, and glowing with fierce anger towards society as a whole. The study here is difficult because it is necessary to fight not with individuals, but with whole egregors, which requires first of all self-denial and internal work, which in this case is also difficult. However, it is precisely these people who can most deeply understand their society, its roots and origins, and see its future in insignificant streams that make their way weakly through the swamp of everyday life, and indicate its development the most promising direction. These people feel the pain of society like no other, they seem to have a magnifying glass built into them, tuned to vices and developmental deficiencies, and the general culture of society is very clearly manifested in its attitude towards them.

The inner world of a person with affected nodes has great developmental difficulties, which greatly depend on the specific position of the nodes in the map. For example, the nodes in the movable cross give too much variability of mental structures, and in the constant - their rigidity. In general, we can say that life develops in such a way that it is necessary to change internally, but this is obtained with great difficulty, and most often the changes go wrong, wrong or at the wrong time. In expressed cases, a person can hate his actual self, perceiving it as a set of obsolete, primitive and base programs and instincts, which leads to deep despair, neurosis and psychosis; and the ideals of development are so high that they are absolutely unattainable. Here, the study proceeds in two ways: eliminating distortions in the perception of the current state of mental reality and reconciling with oneself in the current version or forming a sufficiently high, but realistically achievable ideal, or at least specific stages of development. It requires high internal discipline, achieved through the study of Saturn, and the development of internal honesty, which is controlled by Neptune.

Relationships Between Planets, Houses And Signs

I t is important to understand that there is a deep correlation between the three: planets, signs and houses.

As I wrote before houses are corresponding to signs: Aries - 1 house, Taurus - 2 house, Gemini - 3 house and so on until Pisces - 12 house.

As for the relationships between planets and signs.

Each sign is controlled (dominated) by a certain planet - it is called the owner or ruler of the sign - the most consonant with it in principle. If the planet is in the opposite sign, it is said to be in detriment (imprisoned). For example, Aries is ruled by Mars, therefore, in Libra Mars is imprisoned. In addition, in each sign one of the planets has the greatest power - it exalts. In the opposite sign, on the contrary, it loses its strength or its principle is somewhat distorted; so planet is there in the fall. For example, in Aries, the Sun is exalted, therefore, in Libra it is in fall. Mars is exalted in Capricorn, so in the fall it is in Cancer.

Here is the exalting/falling table:

Sun: in fall in Libra (exalted in Aries)

Moon: in fall in Scorpio (exalted in Taurus)

Mercury: in fall in Pisces (exalted in Virgo)

Venus: in fall in Virgo (exalted in Pisces)

Mars: in fall in Cancer (exalted in Capricorn)

Jupiter: in fall in Capricorn (exalted in Cancer)

Saturn: in fall in Aries (exalted in Libra)

Uranus: in fall in Taurus (exalted in Scorpio)

Neptune: in fall in Capricorn (exalted in Cancer)

Pluto: in fall in Libra (exalted in Aries)

In the description of each planet I will give you it's characteristics in each sign.

Sun - self identification, conscious position in life, will, personal initiatives, life situations that force native to take action, native's way to present himself to others.

Moon - Perception, emotions, habitual reactions, subconscious reactions, adaptation, socially established patterns of behavior that are written into subconscious structures..

Mars - Action, willpower, planet of warriors (soldiers), direct fights.

Venus - Desires (as in wishes), feelings, love, art, beauty.

Mercury - Analysis, intelligence, interactions, contacts, short trips.

Jupiter - Development, community values, wealth, law, social goals.

Saturn - Limitations, control, discipline, time, age.

Uranus - Unpredictability, reformations, eccentricity, turned to future, .

Neptune - deep unconscious processes, faith, fantasies, hallucinations, ideals.

Pluto - Power, collective will, transformation, forces of nature, deep powerful flows of anything.

North Node In Aries - South Node In Libra
Warrior Is Always Alone On A Battlefield.

This native is born to study the very basic lessons of self-awareness.

In his past incarnations he was too busy thinking of his loved ones. This brought him to the state of indecisiveness and gave him a strong habit of hesitation in every more or less conflicting situation. Therefore this native is not formed as an individual.

He is trying to balance everything around him - opposite ideas, people or situations. He is often putting himself in a position of arbitrator, he is trying to be a fair judge, but because he still doesn't understand himself it is difficult for him to actually do anything.

On a low level of mastering this native is always making himself a buffer between conflicting sides, always trying to bring both sides to balance, always hesitating to make a single decision, hoping that time will pass and he will not have to choose a side.

His self sufficiency, his self confidence can be easily broken because in his past lives he was evaluating himself through the success of his loved ones. So now - as he is not aware of what he actually is - he continues to evaluate himself through others.

His wishes don't manifest because they are mixed with the necessities of others. This leads him to depressions and energy losses. Drains him.

He is torn apart between people and opinions and at some point the situation will become so critically painful that he will be forced to reach to his North Node in Aries. He will feel that it is the only way for him to actually survive.

Here starts his journey to himself. He will gradually learn how not to be afraid to accept a certain point of view and defend what he believes to be true. He will study how to be himself and not the extension of other. Here his previous incarnations will help him to stay in the loving way and to keep his intensity at bay.

This native needs to study how to stay alone from time to time. How to make is heart listen to his head, how not to melt instantly just because someone paid him some attention.

Of all Nodes positions this one is probably one of the hardest as native has very little experience of studying and understanding himself (if any).

He needs to find out who he is, what he brings to the world. What seeds he will put in the soil, how will he defend the sprouts of truth.

House where the native's South Node is placed will show where his identifying with others came from and how it was preventing his growth.

House where native's North Node is placed will show the place where his individuality is born..

In the end he will find himself discovering something amazing - his ultimate truth. And he will suddenly understand that it was there all along.

North Node In Leo - South Node In Aquarius
Only One True King Can Sit On The Throne

In this incarnation native learns how to develop his personal strength.

More often than not he is going to find that he has no one to rely on. To realize that if his life is going to be better - it can only be done by himself, on his own.

His past incarnations left him attracted to the others - his friends, his social groups. Now he feels that people abandon him when he needs them most. This is his first lesson to learn in order to be able to create his own life - there will be no others no more.

Others will be necessarily absent when native is experiencing most stressful moments of his existence. He will have to go through long periods of loneliness, isolation, and in many cases hermiticim

Absolutely capable of strong leadership, in this iisncarnation native must learn to overcome his doubts. His past desire for friendships has to be dropped as it weakens him, weakens his self confidence. He needs to understand that his isolation is exactly the time when he is collecting his powers so that when he finally makes his decision - nothing can divert him from his nature, from his fate.

During the period of low-level mastering this native is prone to great energy losses due to his tendency to ask others for advice and opinion. He is not going to follow that advice anyway, but the energy will be lost while getting it and trying to comprehend it. Following his own goals, his own agenda is the only way to stabilize his energy flows and remain balanced.

From his past incarnations he still has his ability to have friends from all societal levels. Now it is going to help him to know "his" people, help him to become a wise king. But he must never cling to the opinions of others.

When his determination is well rooted, there will be no more distractions on his road to success, as this native can not and most importantly must not be satisfied with something of second-rate. Therefore natives with this Nodes position are often able to find their way from poverty to wealth. This comes when their tendency to get distracted and lose focus is transformed into ability to observe.

Focus against diffusion. In his past lives he experienced lack of control, so now he has a tendency to waste his energy on many useless projects. Until he will understand that nobody is going to control him but himself. When the focus is regained this native will be able to do things that will not only serve himself but the whole humanity.

North Node in Leo is calling this native to find out what is worth living and dedicate his life to it. His principles will become unshakable, priorities will become straight and he will finally realize that he is creating something meaningful and substantial. He himself and also others will later on be able to use this principles as a verified guidelines.

The activity of other people reminds him of his own past incarnations.

He wants life to move in a direct course, and at the same time wants to maintain his full independence.

As a result, it is difficult for him to tolerate other people who are constraining his style - he will constantly check the limits.

He is amazed and fascinated by all the possibilities that are available to him and people in general.

At the same time, he is annoyed when he sees people clinging to their own limitations, because he knows for certain that it is in one's power to expand.

His current task is to learn how to implement Aquarius's genius, his individuality in the practical and shiny Leo's manner. His unique beauty now gets a real chance to be manifested. And here will come another challenge - he has to learn how to be alone in the crowd. As without a crowd, without an audience there is no act, but truly unique individual can only be raised in solitude.

This native may spend later years of his life alone or at least keeping his family members on the periphery of his circle as he will finally develop a habit of self sufficiency and realize it's value.

House of the South Node will show a sphere of life where native's needs for originality and freedom are still looking for expression.

House of the North Node will show a sphere of life through which all the energy of native's chart can be focused on a significant new radiant creation - a gift of generosity to the world.

North Node In Scorpio - South Node In Taurus
The Cockswain Must Not Be Bothered About The Shore

This native must learn to accept change and transformation.

His past incarnations left him tired and now he always feels that he would like to finally rest and enjoy the fruit of his labor. He is constantly looking for some stability, some peace. As a result he is clinging to the old patterns that were serving him well in his previous incarnations. He got used to put enormous effort into everything he have been doing before and - just like a bull - he is moving through his present life slowly as if it is a long straight furrow. He now gives so much attention to his physique that his spiritual self weakens.

Native with South Node in Taurus feels that he has to study everything on his own so he often neglects knowledge of others, prefers to build his way all by himself, thus creating an illusion of stability in his life.

Deep level of transformation is essential for such native to reach his North Node in Scorpio.

He needs to destroy his old habits, burn all bridges behind him, to cut all ties cleanly and properly so that he will enter his future without his old luggage.

This position of Lunar Nodes shows a soul that was living in decay for many incarnations and now it needs to get rid of everything that was collected before. Native has to be prepared to lose everything and he will probably lose more than he expected.

Some natives with North Node in Scorpio spend their late years in a complete solitude as in the process they dropped everything except themselves.

House where the native's South Node is placed will show where the native's decay comes from.

House where the native's North Node is situated will show the path of transformation and rebirth in the current incarnation.

When native learns how to drop everything he once possessed - from this symbolic death - his new life will finally emerge.

North Node In Capricorn - South Node In Cancer
To Lead Is To First Follow

This native must learn how to reach maturity.

In his past incarnations he was driven by his emotions seeing only what he wanted to see, forgetting that there is much more to the existence than his immediate environment.

South Node in Cancer lives native with the feeling that he is still a child struggling with his subordinate position. His growth is often sabotaged by his past childish habits. South node in Cancer is pulling him backwards by giving an inner need to find a parental approval and attention. And more - by tempting native to give all responsibility to someone superior (a parental figure).

At the low level of mastering native wants to keep himself away from responsibility at all costs. Often this may result in a disease that natives develops to get maximum attention while justifying his own inaction (you see how ill I am - how can I do anything in this situation? I need help, I'm disabled).

From his past incarnations such native brings a constant feeling of being incompetent - he always doubts his practical skills, his actual physical abilities. Cancer is a very feminine sign so inaction is one of the strongest pulls against native's development. And this is the reason for such native to cling to his country traditions, to his patriotic feelings as those are able (that's how he feels) to relief him from the unbearable burden of making his own responsible decisions.

Often South Node in Cancer gives native a feeling that he has to preserve as much as he can. Fear of forgetting something. So he is collecting millions of memories thus making himself a huge cosmic attic, preserving things that are of no use. His love for past may prevent him from finding out what actually is going on with him right now.

The main mission of a native with North Node in Capricorn is to be able to identify himself with something bigger than life - a greater ideal. Saturn (Capricorn's ruler) is calling him to attain the timeless. The crystallized perfection. He needs to find out what' right and then stand for it - regardless of what other's sbelieve. His goal is to understand what is the real responsibility.

Mastering the North Node in Capricorn creates an ideal that others can worship. Native himself becomes a perfect system that others can follow. He himself becomes a tradition that is not just a mere fairy tale but a deep personal experience step by step verified by time and responsible effort.

House where the native's South Node is placed will show where the native's immaturity comes from.

House where native's North Node is placed will show the way to a responsible mature existence.

When such native learns how to attain maturity with honor, transparency and with respect and mindful use of tradition - his brilliancy becomes available to him.

North Node In Pisces – South Node In Virgo Tell God About Your Plans And Watch Him Laugh

These natives were spending lifetimes collecting knowledge and trying to understand how everything works. At least that's what they thought they were doing. And now they are born with deep conviction that the universe is limited and well structured. Now they are destined to realize that existence goes far beyond any limits that can be measured or even understood by human mind.

During the first years of his life native with North Node in Pisces is still looking for order.

His need for strict regulation is so strong that rigidity and ossification in the body may even increase pressure on the internal organs.

He constantly suppresses desires in order to do what seems right, as he would like to maintain an image of respectability.

In his past incarnations this native was building his understanding on facts that had to be confirmed by his empirical experience and by empirical experiences of others.

Now he is ready to agree with and to recognizes only that which comes from any sort of "higher authority."

He is looking for ways to free himself from the nervous excitability that continues to sweep and exhaust him, but in the same time he wants to sets the conditions for his treatment himself on his own terms.

Over and over again this native inevitably encounters situations, circumstances and events that force him to "lose the physical plane".

Nevertheless, he still tries to live against the flow, to move according to his intellectual understandings and regardless of the direction of the natural forces.

His past life habits makes him now suspicious and always willing to disassemble what should be left together. This native spends hours looking for an answer, but he can get so involved in the process itself that often loses perspective. Thus, although he is capable of extreme clarity of thinking, he does not experience complete peace of mind.

When his perfectly designed plans will one after another turn into nothing, he will begin to see other things and people in a different light. He will inevitably go through experiences that will force him to become open to the oneness, to stop dividing the world into neat little pieces.

While this native is still clutching at the restrictions that he himself imposed, the new desire is growing within - he is looking for a higher alternative. North Node in Pisces is calling him to experience faith.

From time to time, his wonderful intuition given by Pisces reveals to him the mysterious essence of being, but the memories of the past incarnation - of the practical Virgo - will make him doubt everything. His inability to completely free himself prevents this native's transition to the full state of a higher mind. However, he reaches the point at which he can sometimes see it. Thus, halfway between one world and another, these mutable Nodes are in constant change. Arriving at the destination, this native is never sure that he is in the right place, and therefore he continues to come back to begin his journey again.

Each time he takes one more step to infinity, where in the end he will finally be able to dissolve the chains of his rigidly formed past and will be born again as a pure Spirit.

House of the South Node will show a sphere of life that is still too rigidly embedded in an overly structured idea. House of the North Node will show how this soul can open its grip on it's rigid definition of shape and structure so that it can drift freely in the Ocean of God.

North Node In Cancer - South Node In Capricorn Statues Do Not Evolve

This native have spent his past incarnations learning the art of achievement, studying to overcome obstacles in almost ultimate solitude - without not only support but without even much interaction with others.

He is now born to realize that one is never alone. He is now born to learn how to accept support and how to provide support for others and - somewhere on the way - to develop his nurturing and emotional feminine side.

This soul was working so hard in it's past lives to gain recognition. Life after life great goals were set and the ways of achievement were calculated with mathematical precision. Native with South Node in Capricorn comes to this world with a lot of inner pride, expecting respect, valuing prestige more than anything.

In his early years this native will surprise his parents with amazing level of maturity demonstrating unique determination in gaining knowledge, being practical and even tactical in all his interactions. Perfect child! But here lies the trick - the cup of determination and responsibility is full, overloaded to the extent where native can't maintain it in a healthy manner anymore. The hard work of his past incarnations becomes now his fixation, a matter of frozen pride. Now he would like the world to know how burdened he was, so that others could perceive him as a martyr.

He continues to make his work way more difficult than it actually is until he himself cannot cope with the responsibility and obligations of his current life.

Deep inside this native is absolutely convinced in his righteousness and he often condemns the actions of other people. However, he keeps this to himself so that others will not find out that he fits them into his secretly invented caste system.

He perceives everyone and everything through his own filters of what's right, beautiful and worthy. But only until the perfect statue that he had carved out of himself becomes another obstacle on his own way. Only until he is made to realize that his work of achieving perfection is done and now life has to make it's way through that perfect form.

Now the flow of life takes it's course and the statue crumbles under the wind and the rain of evolution to reveal the living soul and the beating heart under the perfect stone. Now the North Node in Cancer is pushing this native on a path where he will learn to hear, see and accept his own human nature and that of others.

Many people with North Node in Cancer are going to be experiencing strong family bonds to learn emotional needs of people around them. Tough principles of Capricorn are going to be destroyed and discarded one by one. New confidence and new reliability has to be found now in a more honest and more open attitude towards one's emotions.

In this life, native must learn to sincerely apologize if he is wrong, and not look for advantages over others if he is right. He will learn how to slowly refuse from the ever hungry need to control everything and everyone. He is now going to develop a new pattern of emotional reactions and let his intuition develop and finally take a rightful place in his decision making.

When this is done native with North Node in Cancer becomes a true cornucopia of spiritual food for those who are hungry.

The more he is able to nourish other people, the happier and the more fulfilled he will become. He will finally come to the realization of a simple fact that God is ready to give to those who don't seek anything for themselves and thus whatever was collected in the past incarnations now has to be given to the others, has to become a nurturing soil for other seeds to grow.

House of the South Node will show a sphere of life where the cornucopia is full.

House of the North Node will show where this native has to fill the empty cups of others in order to become a nurturer of the evolution itself.

North Node In Saggitarius South Node In Gemini Enough Of Looking At The Neighbours Problems

The native is born to venture out in the open skies, where there is no barrier that sets him in chains. In his travels the native performs various mental, emotional and spiritual maneuvers, letting him find people from all across the boundaries of human will and purpose.

The native will be bound again and again by the chores and boundaries of his limited home, it is quite possible for the native to be born in a place where he finds his roots strong yet people at home trying to show him a way out. Parents in general or siblings at home will have a sense of freedom but will lack the courage to step out, and with them they will dream of the open skies.

The native here is being fed with stories of how it is glorious to move out and how great the world is outside. This sense of the outside will make the native want to travel in his early age, from the time puberty locks its weight on the native he/she will want to go out meeting strangers. The native will be quite charmed by people who have a rebellious outlook towards society, who wear loose clothes and find a smoking joint at every nook and corner of the road.

The Sagittarius north node is very interested in others, to a level that they forget to teach themselves. They find out with time that the possible outcomes to a solution are based on the heroics of people that they are trying to influence. Hence he will waste a lot of time trying to influence others and finding a way through the minds of others. This is a very lowly developed native who will have to find the courage to step on the road to wilderness all alone. So the way to development here is to say a no to everything that seems to be clinging on the shoulders of others.

They keep playing mental games, and whenever they see a situation unfolding, they try to work out the logical sequence of events in their mind. In the end they find out that they have been left with the short end of the stick and the real nectar of the fruit has been enjoyed by the people whom he thinks do not deserve at all.

The native is well versed with logics, as that have been his prime focus in his past lives, here he has come to understand the way of the intuition. He has come to learn to trust his guts and to have faith in the playground of his interior cosmic game. He has to learn to have faith that things will unfold, rather trying to work out a logical future in his head and then being the controlling and nagging tamer of his fate.

The game of logic is the game of manipulation, and when the native finds his way out by manipulating others is when he has taken a wrong step forward. Also, he is now being motivated by something that will pull him back further and further.

The destiny of the native is to channelize their optimism, their faith and their intuitive energies into this world. To live by this code and to radiate such energy wherever they go. If they violate their destiny by logically manipulating their opponent, they will soon find an opponent who is stronger than them, and this pattern will repeatedly curse them with new sorts of pains.

In this lifetime, they need to escape the storm and weight of other people's thoughts. They truly want and desire deep inside vitality on a fresh level. They will need to trust everything that gives them vitality, provides them with an energy blast, may it be physically, mentally or emotionally. Their deep desire is to reach to far off lands where they can look upto the sky and say ' AS YOU WISH'.

House/ sign of the south node will show mental struggle, politics, manipulation and sphere of the north node will show intuition, faith, unconditional optimism and relentless freedom from the burdens of one's own mind.